Canvass This!

Canvass This!

Tobias Salinger

Copyright © 2010 by Tobias Salinger

All rights reserved. No part of this book may be reproduced, stored, or transmitted by any means—whether auditory, graphic, mechanical, or electronic—without written permission of both publisher and author, except in the case of brief excerpts used in critical articles and reviews. Unauthorized reproduction of any part of this work is illegal and is punishable by law.

ISBN: 978-0-557-57180-2

Tobias Salinger, 25

1620 Riggs Place, NW

Washington, DC 20009

tsalinger79@gmail.com

816.721.4037

For my friends and relatives

Contents

Chapter 1 1
Chapter 2 13
Chapter 3 23
Chapter 4 35
Chapter 5 45
Chapter 6 57
Chapter 7 67
Chapter 8 79
Chapter 9 93
Chapter 10 103
Chapter 11 115
Chapter 12 125
Chapter 13 137
Chapter 14 149
Chapter 15 161
Chapter 16 175
Chapter 17 187
Chapter 18 199
Epilogue 207

Chapter 1

"When I was One-and-Twenty…"

When I was one-and-twenty
I heard a wise man say,
'Give crowns and pounds and guineas
But not your heart away;
Give pearls away and rubies
But keep your fancy free.'
But I was one-and-twenty,
No use to talk to me.

When I was one-and-twenty
I heard him say again,
'The heart out of the bosom
Was never given in vain;
'Tis paid with sighs a plenty
And sold for endless rue.'
And I am two-and-twenty.
And oh, 'tis true, 'tis true.

-A.E. Housman

When I was sixteen, I spent my summer as a little league umpire. I drove my rusty Toyota out to a little league stadium in south Kansas City on steamy summer nights and pulled in fourteen bucks an hour while I punched out kids half my age. Not literally. I mean I had a large strike zone, and I loved to ham it up, and I used to let out a roaring "HEEE-RIKE THREEE!" as I performed my pompous out signal.

I could tell most of the managers and parents in the league hated me. Eddie Kliensasser, a friend who worked there with me that summer, said there was always some point in the game when the coaches and fans would get pissed and start telling their kids to swing at everything. One time, the coach of the Indians screamed at me because I didn't kick a bat out of the way of a potential play at the plate. His face was blood red and he yelled at me in front of everyone, "You know, at least your partner understands the game!" I just looked at him. Eddie ran in from the infield, his eyes as big as plates.

"You don't have to take that," he told me.

The memory that stands out most is the time I umpired a game Eddie's cousin played in. I knew the kid and his dad and I liked them both. I called what I considered a routine game, but I could hear the dad snickering all night.

"Toby," he said after the game. "You are an odd duck."

--

In the fall of my senior year at Texas, the 2008 election seemed far away. None of its characters knew what roles they would play or what would happen.

I sure as hell didn't know. I cut out pictures of political figures from magazines and mounted them on the walls of my shitty apartment. I would get stoned and stare at them. There was a big, grinning Rudy Giulliani face I found in *The New Yorker* that captured his inanity and hypocrisy. Hillary Clinton loomed all over, hugging old ladies and smiling with Bill and Chelsea. The rest of the field crowded in wherever they could, a gelled Mormon, a beaming evangelical, and a black man. Maybe it was the pot, but the thought of any of them as president made me giggle.

I had other concerns. The notion of jobs crept up on me. I hadn't seen it coming. Like all college students at home during breaks, I used to dread the inevitable holiday conversations with friends of my parents. I cut them short with standard responses.

"So, how's Texas?" they'd ask.

"Outstanding," I would say with an earnest look. Something in my emphasis of the first syllable kept people from asking any more questions. I had it down to a science by the end of my sophomore year. Little did I know that the job queries would be starting soon. I had no answer.

I went to Austin with the idea of becoming a baseball broadcaster. I had loved going to Royals games more than anything else because that had seemed the only thing worth doing in Kansas City. Eddie and I use to drive out there every chance we could. We went to seventy games a year, and I cherished the new circumstance of each day's game as evidence of the beauty and variety of the world. The prospect of being paid to talk about baseball looked ideal to me.

A football game the Longhorns played against Tech my sophomore year smashed that whole idea. It was a sticky fall afternoon and Vince Young dominated, but I hardly paid attention. I had taken sixty shots of beer in sixty minutes and eaten a pot brownie and the game seemed evil. Everyone in Memorial Stadium was wearing the same color and screaming at the top of their lungs about a meaningless contest. When Vince would glide in for yet another touchdown, thousands and thousands of yahoos, including myself, would shout "Texas Fight" as if there were no problems with the world. And then we had a fighter jet fly-over.

"I'm scared of the power of my government!" I shrieked when the roar of the planes had passed. Everyone sitting around me laughed, and I meant it as a joke, but I was also serious. At that moment, the football game seemed an amusement put on for the masses so that we wouldn't think about oppression or torture or the Patriot Act. I thought about a scholar named Hobsbawm I read in my introductory anthropology class who chronicled the manner in which invented traditions benefit institutions. I couldn't take part in a spectacle like that without acknowledging its meaninglessness and I wouldn't participate in anything that I suspected might keep President George W. Bush in power.

Drugs were an integral part of my experience at Texas, I'll be the first to admit it. I doubt anyone who knew me then would be surprised to hear it. I experimented with them not just for their psychological effects, but also because I wanted to rebel against how I thought I was perceived. I remember the time I tried coke with Eddie. We took some lines off an old coffee table and stood around drinking beer and lamenting the fact that there were no parties to "dominate" at four in the morning. I was clicking my teeth together and talking a mile a minute. My nose and mouth felt numb and I couldn't think of anything about myself that I didn't love. At one point I said to Eddie, "I wish everyone who knows me could have seen me do that line."

He laughed. "That's pretty fucked up, man."

Another time, Eddie barged into my room when I was sleeping and asked if I wanted to do some coke. I turned him down but agreed to sit up and talk with him. He couldn't stop talking about jobs.

"You have to get a good job early or else it's almost impossible to get one," Eddie said in a grim tone.

I smiled and told him that I didn't think that was true.

"It's definitely true," he said. "Toby, you might read all the biggest books you can find and get the best grades, but you're going to have to get a job like the rest of us. You think you reject money and institutions, but you're going to be sitting in an office. And it's going to suck."

He began to get animated, so I conceded the point.

Psychedelics were different. They seemed more contemplative, intellectual. Mushrooms produced experiences I'll never forget. The first time I ate them, I circled Pease Park again and again with Eddie and a group of our friends. We kept remarking about how it seemed we were on a vacation from reality, but all we talked about was that we never wanted to leave college and sit in an office somewhere. The park's walking path, we decided, represented the path authority figures wanted us to follow in life. We were too scared to stray.

The shrooms provoked talk about society's conventions. On a different trip, Eddie and I equated life to a spider web while we sat around my room cackling like hyenas. There was nothing my roommate would rather do, he said, than walk around all day in a towel and flip-flops.

"You can do that whenever you want," I told him.

He couldn't, Eddie said. People would be distracted and wouldn't take him seriously. Police would arrest him. Girls would think he was insane and they wouldn't have sex with him. Every time you think you can make a statement by violating the norms of society, he said, you can find a thousand reasons why your message won't come across or why your rebellion is pointless. I agreed that free will is a myth.

Acid was just as enlightening. Eddie and I spent part of our LSD trip at the Thai Noodle House. I was drinking a Thai iced tea and looking at him through my dark green sunglasses when he asked, "It's amazing isn't it?"

"What's amazing?"

"The number of people who have gotten shot for advocating peace." The simplicity of his words was terrifying.

I spent a night in jail. Eddie and some of us were driving down I-35 and passing around a weed pipe when we saw signs for the Alamo. One guy admitted he'd never seen the damn thing, so we had to stop. Unfortunately, we also rolled down our windows. Soon after we pulled off the interstate, a couple of bike cops rode up and started sniffing. The next thing I knew, we were cuffed and bound for the detention center in the back of a paddy wagon. We spent thirteen hours there. Jail is an eye-popping experience for any middle or upper class white boy. The combination of boredom, the frigid temperature of the facility, the hopelessness of the other people who were locked up, and the smug attitude of the staff still haunts me. I never imagined that my freedom could be snatched away so easily and I never knew people could take pleasure in doing it. I still remember how I hated the fat officer who took my mug shot. He kept waving and saying, "Smile! Smile!" I didn't. I vowed never again to be stupid enough to give someone like him power over me.

That didn't keep Eddie and me from lighting up again. My favorite memories were the times we smoked in my apartment after a night downtown on Sixth Street. Eddie was a sight in the bars down there, the way he would show up with as many people as possible and take everyone up to the bar for a shot of tequila. He didn't care if he bought eight or ten of them, he wanted to have a good time and he wanted everyone to be a part of it. Of course, if he had a chance of taking a girl home, he would lose all thought of the group he had toasted minutes earlier. He would focus on her, his face convulsing with loud laughter and unlimited conversation. It worked. Girls would buy into his vigor for celebration like they bought into the way he spiked his blonde hair and the way he dressed in brands they knew. But it didn't work other nights, and he used to devote his energies on those evenings to binge drinking on his parents' credit card. When the bars shut down at two, we would ride the bus back and take bong rips.

One night in particular stands out to me. Eddie had been chasing some sorority girl around that night, and he had done all he could to no avail. He was bellowing and guffawing about the exploits of his fraternity brothers at the last party they threw for the sorority. She was paying attention and laughing at his jokes, so I had assumed Eddie was going to take her home. So did he.

"Man, I thought I had her," he said. I said I thought so, too.

"I know, right?" he asked, looking at me for confirmation. "She was having a good time talking to me. I can always tell when they're enjoying themselves, and she was tuned in to me, man." I agreed again.

"Well, fuck it, man," he said. "Let's just get high." I handed him the bong and turned up the rap music.

"What's with you?" he asked. "You're not saying much."

"It's nothing," I said.

"Oh, come on, man," he said. "You gotta tell me. I know what it is, I know what it always is: you're lonely. You're looking for that girl and you're not finding her. Right?" Eddie let out one of his laughs. "I knew it, man, you're always thinking about that. You want a girlfriend, and you'll find her sooner or later." It was moments like these when a different person from the Eddie who binge drank would emerge. It was this Eddie who was part of the reason I went to those Royals games and decided to go to Texas. He knew it, so I didn't say it.

"You're going to find it and like it, man," he said. "But then you're going to see a different side of women. I know you want somebody because you want to go on walks and weekend trips and shit like that, and that's fine, that's definitely part of it. But there's another part of it, too, the part where women show that they're full of shit."

I said I didn't think that was true of every woman.

"Oh, really?" he said. "How do you know? You can take it from me, man, I've had sex with thirty-seven women." I laughed.

"You're a bit behind Wilt Chamberlain," I said.

"Yeah well, give me a few more years. But that doesn't matter. Let me tell you what matters: you need to work on your demeanor around women."

"My demeanor?" I asked.

"Your demeanor. Look at the way we're sitting and talking right now. You're relaxed and we're speaking without being afraid we might offend each other."

"I'm not afraid I'm going to offend them," I protested.

"That's not what I'm talking about. You always make such a big deal of them when they're around. You're constantly going out of your way to try to see them and you're always the one approaching them. You need to relax and let them come up to you."

"You mean like you were when you were telling stories about the boat party? You would have taken off if you could have flapped your arms any more."

"Oh, please, you know that girl was into me. You know exactly what I mean, and you know that going out of your way for girls like that is bullshit." I couldn't help but laugh at the way he accentuated the "b" sound to make a popping sound at the start of the word. I was taking a class in speech science at the time, and we had learned how every sound in our language is produced by a particular positioning of the vocal folds. We had looked at videos of the folds during enunciation, and, though I never had much interest in science of any kind, I was fascinated by the way minor changes in the air that came through the folds could create sounds that were vastly different. And now, looking back at those days in speech science, I am struck by the fact that I never knew that the vocal folds look a lot like a vagina. I couldn't have because I had never seen one. I laughed in spite of myself that night, though.

I looked like a person who had experienced half-baked epiphanies. I didn't get a haircut for three years, and my hair grew down past my shoulders. Older males of all kind gave me constant crap about it, and I liked that. To my mind, the keepers of these institutions needed to be tormented by a youth who wouldn't fall into line. By my senior year, my hair was so long that I had it braided into cornrows. I also bought the loudest eyeglass frames possible, a shiny metallic red and blue pair everyone noticed. In retrospect, it's not surprising that I never got laid.

With no girlfriends to occupy me, my intellect grew with my hair. The drugs would not have been as enriching without my academic experience. My media theory class about the treatment of minorities on television and film, for instance, posed questions of entertainment versus message in a manner that will give me a critical eye for every program I watch the rest of my life and a critical ear for every phrase I utter. I feel the same way about classes I took on the literature of World War I, the effect of globalization on India, the history of the American Civil War, and others. The summation of all of them seemed that powerful institutions control our society and the world. As a citizen with a choice about whether to set myself up to benefit from hegemonic order or to spend my life fighting it, I felt it my duty to do the latter.

My initial major did not pass the ideological purity test. I started as a journalism major with the intent of becoming a baseball broadcaster. Although my English teacher parents were skeptical of the intellectual vigor of a degree from a communications program, they were satisfied that a journalism program would produce employment. It turned out that I agreed with them. I became bored and exasperated. We were taught that there are only seven ways to begin a newspaper story, and that every story needs a "nut graph" summary, and that, for the purposes of journalistic writing, our paragraphs should be insubstantial fragments of facts and quotes known as "graphs." It always irked me when my professor would instruct someone to cut out a sentence and place it "a few graphs down," as if a piece of writing were a puzzle one snapped into place.

On top of that, I found my classmates dull. They whined about news quizzes that required a simple attention to current events, and they read our textbook as if it were a primer on winning a Pulitzer instead of a pile of self-evident bullshit. They also called me a teacher's pet.

When it was final exam time, a classmate hosted a study party at her apartment. She asked everyone to bring food or drink. Not concerned about a multiple choice test, I brought a case of Miller Lite. To my disgust, I sat there drinking alone as they reviewed every single chapter in a thorough and laborious manner. When the study session ended, one of the girls in the class asked to speak to me in private.

"Have you been smoking marijuana, Toby?" she asked me. "It's OK if you have."

"No," I said and walked away, even though I had smoked two fat joints before I came. Perhaps my demeanor with women needed improving, but I didn't care about this one.

I stuck with journalism anyway and qualified for the Broadcast program. It was to be a three-semester sequence in which we would produce an actual newscast. In the first semester, we put together a news show that ran on student radio. Our professor was a former Fox News producer who enforced what she considered the paradigms of good journalism. I remember one time when we were pitching stories for a show about UT administrative matters. I proposed a story about the increasing competitiveness of the University's admissions process. She wrinkled her nose.

"What's the news peg?" she asked.

"What's a news peg?" I asked.

"Has there been an incident involving admissions, something that makes it newsworthy to do a story about it?"

"The story is that it's becoming almost impossible to get in here," I said.

"That's not a news peg. A news peg would be the release of a study, a new hire in the department, a change in policies. Something that has people talking. Every good story has a solid news peg."

I did the story nevertheless and got an A. I decided to switch majors around this time. Journalism school didn't seem challenging or stimulating, and, worse, I began to feel as if a career in journalism would mean compromising my principles. I wanted to report a different kind of news than what I saw in the mainstream media, and I thought one of the biggest weaknesses of the media was their reliance on established, formulaic approaches to the news.

I once had a polemical professor by the name of Jensen who harangued against a quote he displayed on the overhead the first day of class. It seems a longtime journalist defined journalism as "monitoring the centers of power." This attitude, my professor insisted, is the reason why the mainstream media fails and why it ignores the iniquities of our world. I agreed with him. I think the people with the most influence in journalism are fools. The longtime journalist is talking about monitoring the centers of power as if asking questions at a press conference were the essence of democracy. My professors showed me successful, respectable adults in suits agonizing whether it fits with journalistic ethics to save somebody from a car teetering on the ledge of a bridge. When another human being is about to die, one's profession should never make a difference, especially if one's position were threatened by the fastidious fools of the Society of Professional Journalists. The professionalism of journalism is what helped the purportedly "liberal" *New York Times* sit on the warrentless wiretapping story that could have swung the 2004 election for an entire year. Journalists are good people who work hard, but I wanted no part.

I also didn't want to be the model graduates my instructors use to bring up in class. One day, my broadcast teacher tried to motivate us by telling us how one recent grad of the program just landed a job as a sports anchor in Odessa, Texas. Now, I've never been to Odessa, so I can't speak to the quality of life there. But I'll be goddamned before I find out.

I switched to the humanities program, which allowed me in essence to take whatever classes I wanted. I think my former journalism classmates couldn't understand why I dropped out of the program. Every time I ran into the girl who asked me if I had been smoking pot, she would squint and ask me how "the philosophy thing" was going. It's not philosophy, I would explain. But she asked me that same question every time she saw me. In any event, I felt lucky to have found the program. I was able to sample from the University's wide and rich offerings, and I met far more interesting people.

On the other hand, it didn't bring me any closer to employment. By my senior year, I still had no idea what I would be doing. My friends in the business school seemed to have an interview every day and five offers already, but I wasn't jealous of their prospects. I wanted to do something I believed in and I wanted to work hard. The most frequent topic of conversation in my frequent drug trips may have been jobs, but the second most frequent one was how lucky we were to be in college and to enjoy life with no responsibilities. I enjoyed college and took full advantage of my opportunities at a school ranked near the top in the world in both scholarship and partying, but I knew it was time to move on. It was a strange feeling. I didn't want to go back to Kansas City and I didn't want to stay in Texas, great as Austin is. So I would sit in my apartment and listen to records and get high and try to imagine where the hell I would be in six months.

Chapter 2

From To a Child Dancing in the Wind

> O you will take whatever's offered
> And dream that all the world's a friend,
> Suffer as your mother suffered,
> Be as broken in the end.
> But I am old and you are young,
> And I speak a barbarous tongue.
>
> -W.B. Yeats

I had a surprise for my parents when they visited me in March of my last year in Austin. It was my pleasure to inform them that their son had found a job. I told them over breakfast, and they were proud as peacocks.

Migas and huevos rancheros were fitting fare for such an announcement. My parents had taught me to love Tex-Mex that is extravagant in flavor and restrained in price, and they used to take me out for Tex-Mex as long as I can remember. The problem was that, by the standards they had learned in Texas, no restaurant in Kansas City could measure up. They would dissect the problems at every Mexican restaurant. They enjoyed going to one place specifically to insult it, and they dragged me there once to show me how bad it was. As soon as the waitress put the salsa down, my father dipped a chip and grimaced in disgust almost before he put the chip in his mouth.

"This salsa tastes like Ragu paste," he said, smirking at my mom. "Here honey, try some." Then he moved the bowl of salsa over to her for her to taste it.

"This is terrible," she agreed.

"Isn't it awful?" my dad said, grinning.

"It's pathetic." That's when I would cut in.

"Would you two just enjoy the meal and try not to make a scene?"

"Toby," my dad said. "You don't understand. They wouldn't allow this in Austin." My mom nodded in affirmation.

"Look," he said, "They even have the salsa in the wrong kind of vessel." He picked up the salsa. "This is a soup cup. You put soup or maybe fruit in here, but never salsa. It's not shaped correctly for ease of access. And don't get me started on these chips."

"You're insane," I said.

"He's right," said my mom. "They would never put out a vessel like that at El Rancho." She was referring to my parents' favorite old haunt in Austin, a place called Matt's El Rancho where they make the chips on site and seat you in wrought iron patio chairs for margaritas while you wait for your table to open up. My dad had been ordering a dish called the Chile Relleno con Shrimp Mexicana every time he went there since approximately 1970, his last year of college.

As bored as I sometimes was by their constant allusions to the greatness of their Tex-Mex pedigree, I embraced it. They dragged me down to Austin every spring break to show me what frijoles were supposed to taste like, and I stayed for college.

It was the same with many of the habits and thoughts that made my parents different from what I thought was normal. For instance, when my mom came home from the grocery store, it was understood that I needed to unpack everything she had bought with her and greet each new item with enthusiasm and wonder that she had thought of this item and found it. I don't think other boys did this with their mothers, but I didn't care. When I heard her car come back, I would jump up from the television and prepare myself to acknowledge that she had been thinking of me all day, thinking of what I would like more than anything else and making up a list to make me happy. I thanked her to repay her in some way, but I also thanked her to keep from seeing her the way she was when she felt nobody appreciated her, when she would go off somewhere out of sight and come back with her eyes puffy and full of tears. I would do anything to keep from seeing her like that.

My father wore his strangeness with pride. During the election of 1992, he made us participate in a bizarre wine ceremony with our Clinton/Gore yard sign in front of the whole neighborhood. He held a glass of red wine up over the sign and said a blessing for Clinton's chances on Election Day.

"We are here," he said, "because we have reason to hope once again, thanks to a man from a place called Hope. Bill, we love you and we want you to win. It's been sixteen years and America can see that the wait must end. Boray pire hagaffin." Then he poured the wine over the sign, and I watched it as it streaked down both sides, amazed that an election could turn a successful, respected man like my father into a sacrilegious sorcerer. Little did I know that an election would change me sixteen years later.

The saga of my new job began with a simple trip to a career fair. The university seemed to host them every week. Banners advertising them were posted all over campus, and you could always spot the students who were going to them. They would stand out in their suits amongst the throngs of t-shirts and flip-flops. To my undergraduate mind, they were pathetic figures wearing unnatural, uncomfortable clothing to impress the very people they ought to be offending. I pointed to career fairs as a symptom of what was wrong with our academic system. We were told to read between the lines and to be critical at all times, but career fairs would have us become cubicle fodder. I poked fun at them with my friends and parodied them in my blogs. One time I got stoned and went to a career fair in shorts and a t-shirt for amusement.

Little did I know I would find myself at a non-profit career fair just a few months later, my shirt tucked in and my hair cut short. I was desperate and I had finally seen an ad that piqued my interest. There was less than a semester of college to go and I had no idea what I would be doing. The business school kids had limitless options, but for us scions of the liberal arts there didn't seem to be much. I went to some Teach for America meetings, but I was turned off. There was a corps mentality that I found strange and an emphasis on test scores that my background as the son of two high school teachers told me was wrongheaded. I also had read several articles on Teach for America discussing how the corps teachers are disdained by colleagues who feel threatened and insulted, and distrusted by parents who feel shortchanged and resentful. I scored an internship with the *Texas Observer*, a muckracking progressive magazine, but it didn't lead anywhere. Qualified and experienced journalists are getting laid off everywhere. There's no room for an unqualified and inexperienced one. Sometimes I thought of becoming a firefighter, but I knew that wasn't a serious thought. I wouldn't have fit in well in a firehouse.

The non-profit career fair turned out to be right up my alley. There were several employers I would have been proud to work for. There was a Peace Corps table, an Americorps table, a City Year table, an ACLU table, an AFL-CIO table. Those organizations looked like attractive options and I grabbed brochures from all of them. Yet, it was a group I hadn't heard of that interested me most. I had circulated the entire room a couple of times when I stumbled into Progressive Futures Inc. A bald man wearing an ill-fitting jacket was standing in front of a table with a banner bearing this name. He was birdlike and he sidled up to me when he finished speaking with another student.

"Do you like politics?" he asked me after introducing himself.
"Of course," I said with more enthusiasm than I meant to.

Stephen was his name. His company was a political consulting firm for progressive clients. It worked with the ACLU and Save the Children, but also the Democratic National Committee and MoveOn.org. PFI, as Stephen called it, was going to have an impact on the upcoming election by helping elect Democrats on every level. I gave him my resume and he asked if I had time later that day for an interview. That way, he said, he could tell me some more about the organization and get to know me a little better. We agreed to meet at 6 p.m. at a campus coffee shop. Just like that, I had my first interview.

I arrived at the coffee shop a few minutes early to find Stephen seated at a table upstairs with his laptop in front of him. We made some small talk for a while and then he started asking me questions about my internship at the *Texas Observer*.

"I gotta admit," he said. "When I saw that on your resume, I was like 'That's awesome.'" I laughed and told him I really didn't do all that much around there. I helped the editors with whatever they could think of, but mostly I sat and waited for something to do.

"That can be very frustrating," he said. "Do you feel ready to work hard?" He explained that directors worked sixty to eighty-hour weeks. I told him I was ready to work hard and tired of talking about changing the world without doing something about it.

He asked about my communication skills, whether I liked speaking in front of people. I said I was confident in my public speaking ability. I told him how much I enjoyed giving oral presentations but I didn't tell him about the adrenaline that grips me every time I get to perform in front of an audience. He gave me time to ask questions, and I had several. I asked what PFI did for the DNC.

"Canvassing," he said. "We go door to door and talk to people on the street to raise money for the Democrats."

"So it's fundraising."

"No, not when we do MoveOn stuff."

"Mmhmm." I nodded, even though I had no idea what he meant by "MoveOn stuff."

I also asked where I'd be working if hired. He didn't know. PFI already had offices in big cities and university towns, and it would be moving into the swing states. He asked for my preference. I didn't have one, I said, as long as it wasn't Texas or Missouri. Stephen seemed to like that answer. I couldn't think of any more questions, so we shook hands.

"Nice to meet you, Stephen," I said.

"Awesome to meet you," he replied with smiling enthusiasm.

Stephen emailed me the next day to set up a second interview with someone who worked in Denver. I was excited. I remember thinking about the opportunity that was presenting itself to me while I was jogging one day. It reminded me of something my trotskyist high school history teacher had told our class about Lenin. According to him, Lenin thought of nothing but revolution, so that when he drank, he was drinking it, and when he ate, he was eating it, and when he breathed, he was breathing it. He kept his body in shape his entire life in order to be prepared if the revolution started tomorrow.

Now, I had no interest in starting a revolution. I wasn't naïve, or even arrogant. But I had visions of grandeur. The Democratic primary had yet to be decided, but at that time in late March, Barack Hussein Obama had a clear path to the nomination. In all likelihood Progressive Futures would be a chance to help elect the first black president. I would get a chance to win back the White House for the Democrats or know that I did everything I could for them. I had a chance to rectify every one of my cherished ideological tenets; I wanted to do it.

The second interview went just as well. I spoke for a half hour or so with another PFI manager. He asked me the same questions. I had some better answers this time. I didn't mention Lenin, but I told him that if I ever wanted to quit I would just think about the other side. And I told him that I believed this election would be remembered a long time and I wanted to be a part of it. The guy was satisfied with all my answers and he asked me if I had any questions. I asked him about housing in whatever city where I'd be working.

"It depends on where you go," he told me. "In 2006, we had some people working for MoveOn who stayed in wealthy MoveOn donors' houses. They were staying in some mansions."

That sounded great, so I didn't have any other questions. The Denver manager scheduled a third interview for me with a woman in the national office in Boston.

That interview, it turned out, was a formality. The national recruitment director, let me know that I had gotten the job. She asked if I had any questions. I did, but she didn't have any answers. Progressive Futures didn't know when or where I would be working. They didn't know when I would know where I would be working. They didn't know when or where I would go for training. And they didn't know what my living situation would be.

"We work with you through the whole process," she said. "At the very least, you'll have a couch to sleep on."

None of this mattered at the time. I had a job, and it was something I cared about. The details didn't concern me. I was ready.

Stephen called a couple of weeks after I was hired to ask if I wanted to have a beer with him. We met at a dive bar near the UT campus, and he was socially awkward. For one, he ordered a pear cider, paid for it, then looked at me and asked me what I was getting. When we had finished our glasses, I got up and offered to buy him a drink with my next Dos Equis. He declined but bought himself another cider. The conversation was alternately forced or disconcerting. We made small talk about politics, but we also touched on the Austin City Limits music festival. I mentioned how much I had enjoyed the previous year's festival, and he had been there as well. His head was bare perhaps from some kind of medical treatment and he walked with a noticeable limp, so I had a tough time picturing him there in the heat and the sweat and the dust. But he talked about seeing the Indigo Girls, who were one of the groups performing at last year's festival.

"My friend didn't want to see the Indigo Girls," he told me. "But I said to him 'Hey let's do something faggy.'"

He paused as if waiting for me to laugh. I didn't.

"I'm gay and so is my friend, so we always joke around like that," he said as if for explanation.

It was a strange experience, and then Stephen gave me a ride home. His car was a beat up Oldsmobile and it made sputtering noises as he drove it up a hill towards my apartment.

"It always makes that sound when I have passengers," he said. That time I laughed.

It was difficult to tell my friends and family about my job. Most people haven't heard of the political consulting business, and not one person had heard of Progressive Futures. The simple response for the uncomfortable queries was not available to me. Most of my friends knew what city they would be moving to, what their position would entail, and what their daily lives would look like after graduation. I knew none of that. When I told my relatives about my job, one of my older cousins looked worried.

"Be careful," he said. "That sounds like canvassing."

"Oh, it is canvassing," I said.

"Well, that's okay," he said, retracting himself because he could tell I was excited about it. "It's just hard work, that's all."

I did some research about Progressive Futures. My google search turned up references to a couple of lawsuits brought against the company in Oregon and California. The company required people to work more than forty hours a week while paying less than the states' minimum wages. One of the lawyers for the plaintiffs was quoted as saying that it was ironic that a company trying to advocate for progressive change treated its employees so poorly. I also ran into a book called *Activism, Inc.*, which is a pretty good play on PFI's name. I didn't obtain a copy, but the college professor who wrote it decried the influence of companies like Progressive Futures for preying on the ideals of young people and achieving few results.

None of that was comforting, but I did get to meet some future colleagues. A couple of directors flew into Austin one time in the late spring to recruit college kids to be summer employees. I got a call from Stephen in the morning asking me if I could show them around the campus, and they arrived in the afternoon. They were easy to spot, a couple of guys my age pulling rolling suitcases behind them. I suggested we walk to my apartment so that they could set their suitcases down, and I offered them both some ice water, which they accepted and drank like they had just walked across the Sahara. One of them noticed the bong I kept out for ease of use. I asked if they wanted to take a couple of rips and they accepted. We sat down and they talked about working for Progressive Futures. One of them told a story about a time a guy whose door he had knocked on for the ACLU. Apparently, the guy started the conversation berating the ACLU but ended up being convinced to make a $50 donation.

What I remember most about talking to these two directors is their clarification of my job duties.

"You don't know what you'll be doing?" one of them asked me.

"You'll be running an office," the other said. "You'll be in charge of a staff of thirty or forty people, and it will be your job to add up the money everyone raises and hire and fire people." It could have been something in his voice or in the pot, but the idea of that sort of leadership hadn't struck me before then. I would be running an office. I liked the sound of that, but there was no way I could have understood what that would entail both in toil and triumph.

But we had work to do. They brought 750 posters with them with the idea to put up 250 a day. I needed to show them the best places. As we were walking up to campus, one of them took out a staple gun and started putting up the posters on every telephone pole. "Campaign Jobs to Elect Obama!" the yellow placards screamed, advertising for information sessions to be held on campus for the next three days. When we came to a kiosk, they plastered them on top of other posters. Then I showed them to the communications building and to a liberal arts building. Not only did we put up posters on every wall, they also went into classrooms on every floor and wrote the info session times on the chalkboard. These guys meant business.

I enjoyed meeting those guys. They shared my interests in politics and pot and they were passionate about their work. I felt a lot better about Progressive Futures after that day.

I spent the next few weeks negotiating about when I would come to a training. I was a complicated case because I would be traveling during June and they didn't know whether they wanted me to go to training and then start a month later. I wanted to resolve the situation to figure out when I should move out of my apartment in Austin, so I would try to call her every few days or so. I could never reach her, though. She would call me back every several days or so later with no information to report. Progressive Futures didn't know for sure when or where the training would take place, and she didn't know when she would know any of that information. Finally, I got fed up and emailed her to say in a polite way that it was unfair to keep me in limbo. She responded a week or so later to let me know that I could train in July when I came back from traveling.

All I had left to do was graduate. I celebrated with everyone for the last time and said my goodbyes as well as I could. I had the pleasure of reciting a poem I wrote at the liberal arts commencement ceremony in the Erwin Center in front of a few thousand people. The poem was about Vince Young and the graduating class's time at Texas and optimism for the future, and I slicked back my hair and gesticulated wildly and felt an indescribable rush.

I'll never forget the final days in my apartment. I had the feeling of a racehorse at the starting gate. I wanted to be let loose on the world, to agitate for political change, to labor for something I believed in.

Chapter 3

From At the Crossroads

You to the left and I to the right,
For the ways of men must sever-
And it well may be for a day and a night,
And it well may be forever.
But whether we meet or whether we part
(For our ways are past our knowing),
A pledge from the heart to its fellow heart
On the ways we all are going!
Here's luck!
For we know not where we are going

-Richard Hovey

I got word from Progressive Futures Inc. that training would be in Washington, D.C. starting on July 10. They emailed me plane tickets and directions to a hotel in Georgetown and instructed me to be ready to work hard.

I went to one last Royals game before I left Kansas City. One of the players had recently called the team "a bunch of fucking babies" and my old boss came with me to witness the carnage. We've been close ever since she employed me as a frozen-custard scooper back in high school. She's one of those strong women with the good sense to yell at you and the righteousness to make it sting. Her respect means as much to me as anyone I've ever known.

"Be careful," she said. "November is a long way away." I agreed, but I never could have anticipated how right she would be. She also said something that got under my skin. She told me she probably wasn't going to vote.

"That's nonsense," I said. "You don't mean that."

"I do," she said. "I wanted Hillary to win the nomination, but I was ready to get behind Obama. Now it looks like he doesn't know what the fuck he's doing." Many observers would have agreed with her. At this point in the election, it seemed to some that Obama was moving away from any liberal positions one might have attributed to him. He had recently voted to give immunity to telecom companies that cooperated with President Bush's warrantless wiretapping and talked of "refining" his position on the war in Iraq. I didn't care.

"You think you're better than everyone else?" I asked her. "You think you get to avoid picking the lesser of two evils? That's the only choice we have. If you don't vote, you forfeit the only choice you get to make." She laughed, but she wouldn't relent. She did say, however, that I might be right when I told her she would feel differently in November.

A few days later, I was on the plane to D.C, wondering what was ahead, what my colleagues would be like, and whether we would win or lose. I was reading *Seize the Time* by Bobby Seale and I loved the thought of working hard for the next four days and the next four months. I realized that what I had learned in college was, as Seale would say, a bunch of jive intellectual esoteric bullshit. I wanted to stand up and do something, and here was an opportunity to do everything I could to elect Barack Obama. Huey Newton's idea that politics is war without bloodshed and war is politics with bloodshed will stay with me for the rest of my life.

The whole training will not. We were bombarded with information, and I met far more people than I could ever remember. But, by the end of those four days, I had a better idea of what the next four months would look like.

Vern Phillips began the training with a short background about Progressive Futures. He's an affable middle-aged guy who is PFI's national canvass director. PFI started in 2004 as the canvassing operation for the Democratic National Committee. Part of the 750,000 new donors the party attracted in that election were due to PFI's efforts, and Vern said Howard Dean's rise to the leadership of the DNC is attributable to Progressive Futures. Dean had appeared at the last PFI director training conference, but he was unavailable for mine. After the disappointment of 2004, PFI started a series of issues campaigns, canvassing for the ACLU, the League of Conservation Voters, and Save the Children, among other clients. In 2006, Progressive Futures again raised money for the DNC, placing canvassing offices in more and more college towns and on the coasts. PFI also worked with MoveOn.org in 2006, organizing volunteer phone banks and get-out-the-vote efforts. In 2008, PFI would be using tested methods to bring it all together.

According to Vern, we were an integral part of the DNC's strategy for the upcoming election. He showed us the internal PowerPoint presentation that outlined the DNC's plan for winning in 2008. The slide show revealed the party's attack strategy for John McCain. It was simple. "McSame" would be a third Bush term, he was a wishy-washy insider, and he was too old. They planned to pound McCain for supporting Bush on 95 percent of bills in the past year, his remark that the Iraq War might last 100 years, his reversal on the Bush tax cuts, and his inability to understand a 21st-century economy.

The presentation revolved around a new emphasis on person-to-person contact. The party could reach voters by television or radio, traditional phone banking, direct mail, or the Web, but it wanted to reach them in person. The DNC had performed a multitude of studies acknowledging that in-person voter contact is the most efficient way to get out the vote. It's not even close. Vern showed us a sample of one study which concluded that the party had to mail six hundred people to secure one vote, call 450 to get a single vote, or talk to fourteen people to make one vote Democratic. With stats like that in mind, the party formulated its "Neighbor to Neighbor" program. The Democrats would lean on volunteers to deliver the election. Using a sophisticated party database, volunteers would be asked to visit their neighbors twice before Election Day to ask them which way they would be voting and to remind them to vote if they were planning on voting the right way.

Once these voters went to their precincts, the DNC wanted to ensure that their votes would be counted. To avoid a Florida in 2000 or an Ohio in 2004, the party started an "election protection network." The plan was coordination among volunteering lawyers in all fifty states to investigate every state's election code and to plan for contingencies on Election Day so that there would be no surprises. There would be a hotline for any possible voting violations, and the lawyers would be on call to press for lawsuits at any time.

The plan appeared sound, and Vern said we would be the party's "first line of defense." We would be signing up donors to fuel the engine, creating a buzz by starting conversation trees, and encouraging more and more people to become personally invested in the election.

Throughout the training, our supervisors did not fail to acknowledge that we would be fundraising, but they rejected any connotations associated with it. At one point, I asked one of our trainers, Dan Blackledge, whether we could motivate people in our office to do anything else besides raise money. Of course you can, he said, but that's not the point.

"I've been bitching for fifteen years about the way Democrats have run campaigns, but they're finally doing it right," he told me. "We should take pride in being a part of it. Obama will not be president if he doesn't win Pennsylvania, but he won't win Pennsylvania without us."

I had met Dan while waiting for the shuttle to the hotel. While I was admiring Obama merchandise being sold at a makeshift stand right next to the Metro stop, I noticed a guy my age in a pink Obama hat eating a bag of greasy potato chips and staring at me.

"You've never seen anything like it, huh?" he asked. "Me neither. It's probably because no candidate has ever been so arrogant as to make himself into a logo. I'm Dan Blackledge, and I hate Barack Obama." He wiped his hand on his shirt and stuck it out to me.

He said he was the canvassing director of the New York City office, and the best canvasser in the world. Dan told all the new directors that he was the best. I could tell it was some kind of a shtick designed to make people see what it took to be a Progressive Futures director. This swagger, combined with his dislike for Obama, turned a lot of people off, but I liked him because he never said anything commonplace. He had been a strong supporter of Hillary Clinton and he explained one night at dinner that he still couldn't stand die-hard Obama supporters.

"Have you ever spoken to one of them?" he asked. "You can't question anything about him. You bring up the fact that he's connected to a corrupt real estate developer, and they wax poetic about a new era in American politics and we should forget the pessimism of the past and embrace the future and blah blah blah until you want to strangle them for embracing clichés instead of policies. It's bullshit."

"So why are you wearing that hat?" I asked, smiling. I hadn't seen him without the pink Obama cap on at any time.

"Because I'm trying to make a point, the point that this man has made politics in this country so ridiculous that a politician can have a recognizable logo, and that logo can be reproduced cheaply onto a shitty pink hat. I would compare myself to Warhol reproducing Marilyn Monroe's face everywhere."

"But you're still supporting him by wearing the hat, and you're still working for a group that's trying to get him elected," I said.

"That's because I hate Bush."

There was a lot to buy into, a sense that this election could be a turning point. Vern Phillips showed us a study concluding that if young voters voted the same way for three elections in a row, they would vote the same way for the rest of their lives. Young voters backed Kerry in 2004 and Democrats in 2006, so if they went for Obama in 2008, they would be Democrats for life. The vision was Rove-like in its audacity, but it planted the seed in my mind of a lasting Democratic majority.

I wasn't the only one. There was an infectious energy among the forty or so new directors at the training. I roomed with a guy who had just graduated from St. Lawrence. He was as fond of beer and a night as me and he enjoyed talking politics as much as talking sports. Many of the trainees were recent college grads. Some were former lawyers or law students. Some were Peace Corps alumni. Many were homosexuals, to the point where I realized one should not assume anyone's sexual orientation.

I spent one night sipping wine with a couple of the women in the group. The rest had ventured out to see the monuments, but I wasn't especially interested in seeing them for the fourth time. I ran into Maggie and Chavonda in the lobby. We bought some wine, and Chavonda invited us upstairs to her room. We talked about what we were learning and what offices we might be sent to, but then we started talking about poetry and love. I knew something of the former but nothing of the latter. Chavonda was a beautiful middle-aged black woman with long dreadlocks and she smiled and told me that I must be an Aries.

"How did you know?" I asked.

"You have a sweet aura," she said. "All Aries have that." I pay no attention to astrology, but it was a special moment to me. I didn't care that I couldn't figure out whether she and Maggie were lesbians trying to get rid of me. I was out on my own with no reputation and I was learning how I was perceived. Also, there were plenty of other women around. I was impressed with all the women I met at the training. They were strong and intelligent and they were gorgeous. They were different from the girls I had known at Texas. They were outgoing where girls at Texas had seemed prisoners of their comfort zone, and they were ready to talk about the world where girls in college thought I was weird for bringing up topics like inequality. I vowed to have sex for the first time before this election was over.

Based on training, though, I might never have time for sex. Fourteen-hour days would be common and weekend work would be the rule. Running a canvassing office would entail tasks that I could not have imagined. We would be interviewing and hiring people, tabulating and processing the funds our offices raised, and creating and compiling a head-spinning number of spreadsheets. On top of all that, we would be canvassing every day. They crammed trainings for all of these duties into just four days. It was a dizzying amount of information, a microcosm of what life would be like for the next four months.

The training shed some light on my own hiring process. Adam Jacobs, another trainer, taught us that our interviewing would not be so much interviewing as motivating.

"Anyone can canvass," he said. "If you can form coherent sentences, you can be a great canvasser." Therefore, we were instructed on the finer points of recruitment. We needed to conduct three interview sessions a day, blanket neighborhoods with posters, and answer the telephone with gusto. When people arrived at the office, we needed to sign up as many as possible. We needed to connect on a personal level. When prospective employees came in for an 11 a.m. interview, we were told to ask them to start the same day at 2 p.m. The "interview" itself consisted of a short information session about Progressive Futures and an even shorter one-on-one interview. We would ask the interviewee what they thought of the background information, why they wanted to get involved, and what their sales pitch would be for a DNC donation. Then, we would give them a personal compliment to tell them they would be perfect for the job and to show them that we were listening. They would be invited back for an observation day, with a chance to make the permanent staff if they raised enough money on their first day.

It was strange to learn how to hire people to be canvassers considering that I had never canvassed before. Our trainers also taught us how to canvass. Canvassing, Dan told us, is based on basic skills. He narrowed it down to five elements: a friendly greeting, a compelling rap, a clipboard handoff, a positive close to every interaction, and a willingness to work hard. I already knew how to greet and say goodbye, how to hand over a clipboard, and how to work hard. The rap was all I had to master. A rap is what canvassers call the script they recite. Progressive Futures had worked with the DNC to create a standard script, and the trainers handed copies of it out to all of us. Then we practiced it again and again.

"Hi, I'm Tobias Salinger and I'm with the Democratic National Committee," I would say. "At this defining moment for our nation, the DNC and Barack Obama are working hand in hand to keep building the massive Progressive Futures effort that Barack Obama has inspired. Unfortunately, the long primary season left us without much time to prepare for the general election. John McCain and the Republican National Committee have had a three-month head start, and they raised nearly $45 million for their campaign last month. We're going to help elect Barack Obama and the whole Democratic ticket by putting more organizers on the ground, training more volunteers to turn out the vote and getting our message out on the air. But we need to do this right away. What's exciting is that the DNC is going to fund this campaign entirely through individual support, without accepting Washington lobbyist or special interest PAC contributions. That's why I'm out here today. The best way you can support our efforts is by making a suggested contribution of $100 today. This will give us the resources we need to win. The best way to contribute is with a credit card or a check made out to the Democratic National Committee."

After a few hours of studying, I had the rap down and I was ready to go out for my first day of canvassing. One of the trainers took a few of us to the Adams Morgan neighborhood. It's a trendy part of DC with restaurants and nightlife, and the sidewalks were full of passersby. We stood next to a coffee shop, and the trainer told me to start talking to people. I was nervous, but I began to ask everyone, "Do you have a minute for Barack Obama?" Several people were curious enough to stop, and three of them gave me money. All I did was recite the script. I raised $80 for the party in less than an hour. My mouth was dry and I was sweating in the July sun, but it was exhilarating. I had a feeling I would be a great canvasser, and not just because I can form coherent sentences.

Not every part of training was so affirming. Cynicism about Progressive Futures crept into my head and it never left. It started with the constant pep. Many times a day, one of the trainers would give us that maddening "I can't hear you" exhortation, which is supposed to oblige you to shout even louder. I don't know why this makes people yell, and I find it infuriating. I participated in these camp-style cheers as little as possible. I also didn't get a satisfactory answer from Vern Phillips when I asked him in front of everyone about the lawsuits brought against Progressive Futures. First, he avoided the topic. Then, he took me aside and gave me a legalistic answer with no discernible meaning. I felt I already understood the gist of the cases, so I didn't press the matter, but it was disturbing.

I also began to take exception to some of my new colleagues. For one, many of them encouraged the "I can't hear you" cheers. Many of them also smoked cigarettes like chimneys. During breaks, people would smoke two or three cigarettes in fifteen minutes, and I had a feeling that the small minority of us who didn't waste lung and time smoking were seen as square. They would stand in their smoking groups, and sometimes I felt like a kid in middle school who gets left out of conversation cliques. A few of them aroused my dislike because they seemed to have no grasp on politics and could not be mistaken for knowing what they were talking about. One was appointed by our trainers to announce a daily news item for, and, one day, he lauded the adoption of Barack Obama's campaign techniques by the BJP party in India. Most people in the room clapped and cheered.

They must not have been aware that the BJP espouses fundamentalist right-wing politics and constitutes a massive threat to worldwide stability if it gains enough control of nuclear India. I wanted to inform everyone that this was something to fear, but I kept my seat because it is better to be misunderstood than disliked. Plus, Chavonda knew exactly what I was talking about when I brought it up with her later. The same guy stood up a couple of days later to rail against *The New Yorker* cover with the parody of the Obamas as their stereotypes. Most people at training were pissed about that cover, but what I took away from it was that none of them had a healthy sense of irony.

The trainers were capable of ill-advised motivational announcements as well. One showed us a clip of John McCain that was supposed to rile us up because McCain endorsed nuclear power and offshore drilling. In the clip I saw, McCain endorsed both those ideas, but he also declared his steadfast opposition to drilling in the ANWR region of Alaska. This position did not endear him to the right wing, and I had always admired him for it. At least one person agreed with me. My roommate, with the requisite sarcasm, remarked to me that he hadn't been aware that McCain was "the most evil person in the world." Both of us wanted to defeat the man, but both of us were turned off by our team's lack of subtlety.

They pretended to prepare us for every contingency that could come up by having us perform so-called "role plays." During these drills, one person would play, say, a canvasser who needed to be let go while another would be the director who needed to fire them. Most of us had never been in a position of power like this, and we would look at the trainers to make sure that we were not presuming authority that we didn't have. My favorite session was when we learned to deal with canvassers who wanted time off by asking them what specifically they would be doing instead of working and then guilt-tripping them by looking them in the eyes and saying that their canvassing is more important. These role plays were disheartening because it was obvious that PFI believed everyone, even its own employees, could be convinced by the formulaic raps they concocted. The point was not to innovate and encourage but rather to stick to the script.

Adam was the best at this tactic and showed us how to do it. One of the other trainers pretended to be a canvasser asking for time off.

"I'm sorry Adam, I can't make it in on the week of the first, two weeks from now."

Adam looked at the guy blankly. "When?"

"The week of the first, two weeks from now."

Adam sighed. "Why not?"

"I'm going on a camping trip with friends."

Adam acted interested all of a sudden. "Oh really? Whereabouts?"

"West Virginia."

"Wow that's great, I've been camping out there before. Wild and wonderful, that's the state motto."

"Well I'm looking forward to it."

Adam's face changed again. "I can definitely understand, but it's tough to have an impact on the election while you're in a tent in the woods. You're doing such a great job with us that you would maximize your impact on this election by coming in that week instead of going on the camping trip."

"Well, Adam, my friends and I have been planning this trip a long time,"

"Then they'll understand if they have to do some more planning for awhile."

"Adam!"

"Did you hear about the overall goal for our region?" Adam asked as if changing the subject. The guy shook his head.

"Well, I heard the regional director say he's hoping we can bring in $40,000 this week. If we do that over the next two weeks, you could be a part of raising over $200,000 for the cause. We need you here."

"Well, I'll think about it."

"What's there to think about? Can you do this for me?"

Then there was the time that Adam told us about a "swear jar" he had in his office. Every time somebody cursed, they would be required to drop a dollar in the jar. This money could then be used later on to buy treats for the office. The idea that I would be policing the word "fuck" in my office was vexing enough, but I put together something more nefarious at work. The treats were something that we were supposed to buy for our office to be reimbursed by PFI later on. I suspected that this "swear jar" was another way for Progressive Futures to save money. The fact that they not only wanted to do it by keeping people from cussing but also by taxing people who were earning poor wages was disillusioning.

The most frustrating part of training, of course, was the fact that I still didn't know where I would be placed. Many of the trainers asked me for a preference, and I didn't give them any. I said I would go anywhere that I could drink a cold beer after a hard day's work. I thought my response fit in well with the humble Midwestern image I like to cultivate at times, and I believed it too. I wanted to go to the front lines of this election, and I didn't care where that would be. But I was tired of not knowing and frustrated with the lack of organization. It was an inspiring and infuriating time.

Chapter 4

An Old Song Resung

Down by the salley gardens my love and I did meet;
She passed the salley gardens with little snow-white feet.
She bid me take love easy, as the leaves grow on the tree;
But I, being young and foolish, with her would not agree.

In a field by the river my love and I did stand,
And on my leaning shoulder she laid her snow-white hand.
She bid me take life easy, as the grass grows on the weirs;
But I was young and foolish, and now am full of tears.

-W.B. Yeats

Reality set in at one particular moment. Dan was outlining our staff policies, and questions started coming up that were not part of the agenda. He was explaining how health care cost $380 a month out of our salary, how we would get ten days paid vacation upon completion of one year's employment, and how we could expect to earn $24,000 a year before taxes. It was now evident that we wouldn't be paid shit for the work we would be doing.

A new director named Jason raised his hand to ask a question. Jason was one of the real characters of the training. He was a heavyset guy who wore bandannas on his head and capri pants, and he spoke with a lisp. He had one of the most entertaining raps of anyone in the training because of the way he whirled his hands and jumped from side to side during his delivery, and he had used this rap to raise thousands of dollars on the streets of New York. This, time, though, he wasn't going for any laughs.

"I just want to know why I get docked a day's pay when I have to go to the doctor's office," he said. "If I miss a day of work but I still work 80 hours, I get paid so far under minimum wage that it's insane."

Everyone looked back at Dan to see how he would respond. He didn't.

"I don't understand your question," he said.

"I just want to know why that is," Jason said.

"Why you don't get paid for not coming in to work?" he smirked.

"No, I just want to know why there's not some way that all the hours I work during a week can accumulate to make up for the time I lost on a particular day."

At this point, Adam jumped in. He was a favorite with a lot of the trainees because of his humor and enthusiasm.

"We want you to go to the doctor if you're sick," he told us. "If you have to miss part of a day, you won't get docked, and we're here to work with you if you have any questions. But that's not the point. The point is that we're all here to elect Barack Obama."

There were audible sighs in the audience, mine included. It was obvious that the trainers knew there was no satisfactory answer to Jason's questions, and that Adam was making an insulting change of topic. There were murmurs about the terrible pay we would be getting. One of the new directors said to me of Vern Phillips one time, "I just want him to admit that we get paid less than minimum wage." I also remember a moment when one of the real rah-rah people who cheered the loudest when it was Progressive Futures camp-cheer time, leaned over to me and whispered, "We get paid about $4.50 an hour."

All the anxieties of these rumors manifested themselves when Jason asked his question. The room became a cacophony of trainees talking to their neighbors, trying to understand how much we could expect to earn in a month and when we could expect to get our first paychecks. The trainers had to quiet everyone down to regain control of the room. Another new director raised his hand.

"Listen, everyone," he said. "I don't want to be a dick, but we all know what we signed up for. We came here because we wanted to elect Barack Obama, not to collect a paycheck." My roommate later commented to me that anyone who began a sentence by trying not to be a dick inevitably was guilty of being one.

The remark got everyone talking again.

"We're just trying to clarify details about our jobs," I said. "That shouldn't put our loyalty to the cause in question." Chavonda was sitting by me and she nodded in agreement, but most people hadn't heard me because nobody was listening to anyone. Adam called us to order.

"Please, everyone, let me get your attention," he said calmly with his right palm held high like a preschool teacher. "These are completely legitimate questions. You can ask any one of us about them one-on-one, or later on during the training, but we need to move on right now."

During the next break, Adam took me aside to make sure I wasn't upset. I told him the truth, that I did understand what I was getting into, but that I didn't understand why some had to try to silence the discussion. He reiterated that these were legitimate questions and told me that he was my point man if I had any problems.

Adam later informed me where I would be placed.

"We're sending you to Denver," he said as we were walking back to the hotel. I couldn't believe my good luck. I would be working in the city where the convention would be held in August in one of the most important swing states. Adam could tell how excited I was.

"I should tell you that the Denver office is actually a Save the Children office," he said.

"What do you mean?" I asked.

"They're canvassing for Save the Children in Denver, not the DNC."

"But I just got trained for the DNC and I just learned my rap for the DNC."

"There's a different rap. You'll pick it up in no time. Save the Children is a great organization." I didn't respond, and I stood with my head turned away from him as I always do when people give me bad news. I had signed up for this with the understanding that I would be making an impact on a historic election. Now I was faced with the possibility that I would be completely divorced from the process.

"Is anything the matter?" he asked me. I nodded and told him I was set on working for the DNC. I said I wasn't interested in working my ass off for a different cause.

"That's completely fine," he said. "We'll put you somewhere else. Let me make some calls, and I'll get back with you in an hour." I was relieved that I didn't have to press my point. I didn't want to be difficult, but I knew that my desire to help elect Democrats was what got me there, and I knew that I would lose my passion if I did something else. Another trainer who would have been my boss stopped me in the hallway. Adam had told him that I was going to Denver, and he gave me a warm reception. When I let him know I was heading elsewhere, he was similarly supportive.

"Oh, that's okay, man," he said. "I tell them to give me only the best recruits, so I know you would have done great, but if your gut tells you to go somewhere else, do it."

I thanked him and went upstairs to call my parents for advice. My dad answered, but he wanted to get my mom on the phone. He asked me to hold on.

"Emma!" he yelled. "Emma, Toby's on the phone!" I sighed. "Toby's on the phone! Toby! Yes, your son." My parents operated on the nonexistent intercom system which required they scream upstairs and downstairs at one another instead of moving closer.

"Hi Toby," my mom said finally. "How are you?"

"Listen, I just want to give you an update and see what you think."

"Sure, sure," my dad said. "Do you know where you're going yet?"

"Well, that's the thing," I said. "They wanted me to go to Denver to work for Save the Children, but I didn't want to do that."

"Save the Children?" my dad said. "What's that got to do with anything?"

"Save the Children is a great organization," my mom said. I sighed again.

"I'm sure it is, mom," I said. "But I'm here because I want to elect Democrats. I hate that there are starving children in Africa—"

"Toby, they're not just in Africa, they're all over the world and—"

"Emma!" my dad interrupted. "Will you please let the boy finish? Where are they sending you now?"

"I don't know," I said. "The guy who told me about Denver said he would make some calls. But I just wanted to see what you guys had to say."

"Well, I'm not impressed with this outfit," my dad said. "How could they not know where they want to send you?"

A little later, Adam told me that I would be assigned to Albuquerque. I thanked him and I meant it. Albuquerque was exactly what I looking for. New Mexico is always a critical battleground, and I had a few friends and relatives who might be able to put me up. I reminded myself that Gore would have won in 2000 if he had taken New Mexico, and I couldn't wait.

I sat through the final day with a smile on my face because I knew I was going where I wanted. Just before it was time to adjourn, Adam tapped me on the shoulder and asked to see me outside.

"We have a special project for you," he said. "Since you're one of the best here, we want you to be a part of our voter registration project." PFI, he told me, would be registering hundreds of thousands of young people and minorities in the swing states. There would be offices opening up in Virginia, North Carolina, Florida, Michigan, and Ohio, and he wanted me to be one of PFI's first people on the ground.

"This is like freedom summer!" I said. Adam nodded and smiled but his eyes glazed over to betray no knowledge of my reference.

"Where will I be going?" I asked. He told me they didn't know yet because they were still looking for office space. In the mean time, I could work in the D.C. office. I was to report there the next day.

"Well, I guess I could do that," I said, thinking out loud. "Where will I stay here? Can I stay put in this hotel until I'm placed?"

"No, we'll just set you up on someone's couch"

"I know a couple of people who live here, so maybe I could call them. But I'll need to do some laundry." I looked up and I could tell he wasn't paying any attention to my personal dilemma.

"We'll figure it out," he said. "The important thing is that you're on board."

I told him I was.

"Great. If you want to introduce yourself to Ben, he's the national project director." I thanked him and went to go find Ben.

He was sitting in the hotel banquet room where all of our training sessions were held. I went up to him and told him how excited I was to work with him on the voter registration project. He just gave me a blank look.

"I have no idea what you're talking about," he said.

"Well I have no idea what I'm talking about," I replied. "Adam just assigned me to this and said I should come and introduce myself to you."

He sighed and looked around the room.

"Well, I have some idea what you're talking about," he said. "Welcome aboard." He put out his hand to shake, and I tried to ask him some more questions. But he didn't know when the offices would be open, he didn't know where they would be, and he didn't know when he would know. I was starting to get confused, so I got up and left to get ready for dinner.

I tried to explain everything to my roommate, but I didn't understand it myself. I jumped into the shower with a Coors Light and tried to figure it out. He was gone when I got out, so I went downstairs to see if anyone else was in the lobby. I sat in a chair and chatted with some trainees. I hoped to talk to Adam, but he was talking to someone else and there were three other people waiting to see him.

I decided to take a walk around the block. The hotel was in the Glover Park area, and the block around it was filled with gorgeous houses and manicured lawns. The vice presidential mansion is nearby. I admired the houses and stopped to watch part of a little league game going on at a park. The houses and the game appeared so structured and simple compared to my life at that moment. Everyone else knew where they would be next week and the week after, knew where they would be living and what they could afford. The night before, the thought of Albuquerque was so attractive to me. In the process of a few minutes, everything had turned upside down.

I tried to think of the last time anxiety had overwhelmed me. The only time was in high school when I thought I had been rejected from Texas. Everyone told me I had the grades to go wherever I wanted, but Texas was the only college I wanted to go to, and Eddie had already gotten in.

Eddie and I had been talking about going to Texas for four years. I had the feeling that I had accomplished nothing in my puny time on Earth. I was arrogant to think that I was among the best and brightest of my age. Worse, I had dismissed others' anxieties about college admissions in my head because I had contented myself that Texas was a state school that would be lucky to have me. I didn't sleep a wink the night I found out I was rejected.

There were a lot of similarities about my situation that day in Glover Park. I had dismissed others' intense preparations for their employments as if I were somehow above them, as if I knew something they didn't. The job search had made a fool of me like it made a fool of them. I had signed on with this group I knew nothing about, flown halfway across the country, and now I didn't like what I had found.

I tried to pinpoint what it was that was bothering me so much and how I could help the situation. I had no idea where I would be sleeping the next night and no idea how I could get there. I decided I would feel a lot better if I could just fly back to Kansas City and drive back to D.C. It would give me time to get my belongings and arrange for a place to sleep. I resolved to ask Adam if I could drive out to DC instead. I hurried back to the hotel.

On the way in, I ran into Ben.

"Hey, Ben I was wondering if I could--," I began. He stopped me because he had a phone call. He told whoever it was to hold on and put the phone on his shoulder.

"What is it?" he asked, and I told him. He sneered.

"No, you can't. Listen, can we talk about this later?" I nodded and went inside the hotel feeling like a fool. Adam was standing right there.

"Adam," I said. "I'm glad I ran into you. Can we talk for a minute?"

"Sure, but I really need to get going."

"Listen, I'm having some trouble processing all of this right now." My voice started quivering and my eyes started to well up. He gave me the once-over.

"Well, that's part of any political job," He said. "If you can't handle it, maybe this isn't for you." He said the last part very quietly.

"What was that?" I asked, unable to keep my composure.

"It's nothing. Listen, what was the problem?" I told him that I would rather drive to DC than stay here all the way through.

"That's completely fine. Don't worry about it, Toby. It's all good." He smiled. Relieved again, I thanked him. It was mind-boggling. A few minutes earlier, that was out of the question. Now, it was all good. My palms and the back of my neck were sweating, and I stood there in disbelief. I figured I better get over to dinner so I could get a drink. I walked down to the restaurant, which was just a few blocks down Wisconsin Avenue. Adam came up to me right when he walked in.

"We've got to talk, man," he said. "You can't do what you did earlier. You have to be more chill than that, do you understand?" I said I did.

I was ashamed of myself. All my life, I've cultivated a calm demeanor. I want to be the cheerful and dutiful person I am most of the time. Yet, there's something beneath, some sense of desperation. There's another person inside me who rages at the people I feel have slighted me and feels that I am a victim of circumstances. When this person comes out, I lose control of my emotions. It is these times when I feel weakest, and these times when I feel I've let others peer into a part of me that I'd rather keep hidden.

Fortunately, though, these outbursts also lead to me feeling better. When I do let out what is inside of me, there's room for better spirits. Dinner that night was no exception. To begin with, PFI picked up the tab. It was the first and only meal they bought for us. One of the nights earlier in the training, they put out a trough of grilled cheese sandwiches for us along with a cup for us to drop money into to help pay for them. It felt special to be out in a real restaurant on their dime. PFI hired a dj, and we danced like the group of elated drunks we were.

My roommate and I walked back to the hotel together. He asked me if I was going to stay with PFI. It was an appropriate question, given that four of the newly hired directors had quit already and what I had gone through that day.

"I'm going to make it to the election," I said. "What about you?"

"I'm going to work a week or so and see what happens."

We were walking inside the hotel when we noticed Dan sitting at a table outside. There were a bunch of empty beer bottles in front of him, and he was smoking a cigarette. We would have said hello, but it didn't look like he wanted to talk. His hair was all mussed up, and one of his hands was covering his face. When he looked up, we could tell he had been crying because his eyes were puffy and bloodshot.

"What do you think is bothering him?" my roommate asked when we got in the elevator.

I just shrugged.

Chapter 5

Laughing Corn

There was a high majestic fooling
Day before yesterday in the yellow corn.

And day after tomorrow in the yellow corn.
There will be high majestic fooling.

The ears ripen in late summer
And come on with a conquering laughter.
Come on with a high and conquering laughter.

The long-tailed blackbirds are hoarse.
One of the smaller blackbirds chitters on a stalk.
And a spot of red is on its shoulder
And I never heard its name in my life.

Some of the ears are bursting.
A white juice works inside.
Cornsilk creeps in the end and dangles in the wind.
Always-I never knew it any other way-
The wind and the corn talk things over together.
And the rain and the corn and the sun and the corn
Talk things over together.

> Over the road is the farmhouse.
> The siding is white and a green blind is slung loose.
> It will not be fixed till the corn is husked.
> The farmer and his wife talk things over together.
>
> -Carl Sandburg

D.C. turned out to be a straight shot from Missourah. I-70 seemed to last forever as I followed it back east on July 17. I didn't drive my mom's old Rav-4 on any other highway until I reached Washington the following day.

I had piled what I figured I would need for the next four months in the trunk: several duffel bags of clothing, a couple bags of books, and an assortment of tools like my laptop and my weed pipe.

It's strange to pack when you don't know where you're going. I was excited at the prospect of registering voters in a swing state. Of course, I didn't know which state it would be and I didn't know when I would know. That didn't matter to me.

I told my parents I was going to be just like Goodwin and Shwerner. They didn't get the reference, but my mind had already put myself on the SNCC level. I doubt my family put me anywhere close. I could see it in their faces. My parents' jubilation at my employment had turned into unease about my complicated choice.

My dad cooked a Midwestern farewell dinner of t-bones and baked potatoes, and he and my mom tried to convince me not to hitch my wagon to Progressive Futures, Incorporated's star.

"So where will you be going again?" my dad asked.

"Well, I don't know," I reminded him again. "They say I'm going to go to D.C. for a few days while they figure out this voter registration campaign, then they'll send me somewhere else. That's why I wanted to make sure to come back here, so I would have my car."

"When will you know where you're going?"

"I don't know. I figure four or five days, maybe a week. They probably won't let me know until right before I'm supposed to go."

"I think that's shit, Toby," my dad said, as if Progressive Futures were a student of his trying to offer excuses for turning in a paper late.

"Well, there's really nothing I can do about, Dad. Of course I'd like a better picture of where I'll be going, but I want to do this, and I'm just going to have to deal with it." I put a succulent piece of steak in my mouth and chewed quietly.

"But look at you, you've got bags under your eyes, you're drained, you're probably catching cold from not sleeping and eating right. You look like Eddie the morning after a night on Sixth Street." I laughed.

"Well, Eddie always has a good time, and he picks himself right up and goes out to have a good time again. I guess that's the way I'll have to be."

"That's all well and good for college, Toby, but this is the real world, and I don't think you know what you're getting into."

"I think I have some idea."

"No, Toby, I agree with him," my mom said. "You realize that you are going to be out on the street asking people for money?"

"I do realize that, Mom, but that's only for a few days." My dad scoffed at the vagueness of my time prediction. "After that, I'll be asking people to register to vote. I'll be registering young people and African-Americans and motivating them to vote for the first black president. Is there something wrong with that?"

"No, Toby there's nothing wrong with that, it's just-," she put her fork down. There was a look of pain on her face.

"What is it, Mom?"

She shook her head and fought tears.

"What is it?" I repeated in a quieter tone.

"I'm afraid you're going to get your feelings hurt," she said. "You're sweet and you have a great mind, and you think that other people care as much as you do."

"When did I fall, mom, what are you talking about?"

"Oh, she's not talking about you falling all the time," my dad said. "She's talking about the times when you got your feelings hurt because coaches wouldn't put you in for the ballgame or because the choir teacher picked somebody else for a solo. You put so much of yourself into things that you're overly sensitive if you don't get everything out of it that you expect."

I exhaled. "What's that got to do with my job?"

"A lot," my mom said. "You're going to talk to people on the street and try to get them to do something great, but you're not going to convince every one of them, and a lot of people are going to say hurtful things."

"Not even to mention the risks involved," my dad said. "I'm going to be scared for you if you're somewhere in the South trying to register black voters. You realize they don't have laws against concealed guns down there?"

"Well, someone could do that here, too, Dad. I've got to do this, and if some people on the street don't like it, I'll just have to learn to deal with it. What I need from you all is to know that you support what I'm doing." They could tell that I'd made up my mind.

"Of course we do, Toby," my dad said. "We just don't want you to get your hopes up. I personally don't think Obama is going to win." I chatted with my parents about Obama's chances the rest of the night because my insecurities were not a topic I felt like dwelling upon the night before my journey. My parents had raised issues like these with me before. They talked to me about getting my hopes up all the time, but they were so proud of me those times when my high hopes turned out to be well-founded, in a way that suggested they forgot their earlier warnings.

I didn't give a damn about their reservations. It was a chip on my shoulder. I had lots of them. There was Adam wondering aloud if I could handle campaign work. There were powerful interests trying to ruin this opportunity for the Democrats, and powerful people who knew my impact on the election would be trifling compared to theirs. There were fickle girls letting me be a virgin when I was twenty-three. I know the people who underestimate me and put me aside do not feel the enmity towards me that constitutes ill will because I am not significant enough to them to arouse such feelings, but I also know that I have a long memory and that I store up the slights that I feel and use them as motivation to prove those people wrong.

I cruised my Rav straight out of Missourah, and I was in Illinois in no time. Then I was in Indiana and Ohio and West Virginia and Pennsylvania and Maryland and Virginia. America flew past my window, a blur of crops and strip malls. I knew I was there at dusk on the second day, when I found myself on the George Washington Memorial Parkway and I glimpsed the spires of Georgetown through the tall trees and realized cars were zipping by me in the passing lane. My final destination was Arlington, where friends of my parents had agreed to put me up for a few days.

I showed up for my first day of work the next morning, Saturday, July 19th. I had called the office on the drive up, and whoever I talked to seemed to live in an alternate universe. She couldn't conceive that I was driving such a long distance to get there.

"I'm en route to D.C.," I told her.

"Oh great, you should come in today."

"No, I mean I'm driving all the way up there," I said.

"Oh yeah, don't worry we'll be here all day."

"I'm in Illinois."

"Oh really? Well, you should just come in first thing tomorrow."

"Well, I don't think I'll get in tomorrow until late in the day, about seven or eight or so."

"Oh it's OK, you should come in then. You can shadow during cash out."

"Well, it's hard to say when exactly I'll get in. I don't know if I can make it in tomorrow night."

"OK, that's fine. Just come in on Saturday morning for the 10 a.m. directors meeting." So I showed up at the office on Saturday morning. It was on the third floor of a small building tucked away near the Dupont Circle metro stop. I knew how to get there because we had visited the office in training, and I remembered how a long, steep escalator opened up right on the corner of the office's block. The escalator didn't seem as long on that first day, though. When it dropped me off on the street level I had no notion where I was. I looked around and saw Dupont Circle and cars whizzing around it. There was a Krispy Kreme and I could see a CVS off in the distance, but I didn't recognize anything. I called the office and nobody answered. The back of my neck began to sweat in the morning sun, and I looked at my watch. I knew the meeting was at 10, but I had said I would come in at 9:30. It was 9:30 right then, and I was lost. I thought about asking for directions, but I realized I had no idea how to describe the office. I knew I had probably just exited the Metro from the other side, so I resolved to go back down and see if I could find it. When I got back down, I noticed that I would have to go back through the Metro turnstiles, and to do that I would need fare on my metro card. Luckily, there was a station manager nearby.

"Is there a different exit here?" I asked her. She was an older black woman with glasses on the bottom of her nose, and she crinkled her brow at me.

"Huh?" she said as if I was speaking a different language.

"Well, I came here one time and exited right outside the building I'm looking for, and this time, I exited and nothing looked familiar." Her eyes lit up.

"Oh, you went out the wrong side. Here, come through the security gate over here and make sure you go through it on the other side. Tell them I let you in over here."

So I went back through the station, and this time I knew I had it right. But I looked at my watch again as I was going up the escalator. I was five minutes late. The building was a short walk away and I found the door on the left side of Zorba's Greek Café. A doorbell inside was labeled "Progressive Futures, working on behalf of the Democratic National Committee." I buzzed up and someone answered.

"Progressive Futures," said a female voice.

"It's Tobias Salinger. I'm here for my first-" The door buzzed open.

I climbed up two flights of stairs. I recognized a couple of faces from training, and there were a few others I didn't know. Adam Jacobs was there in a polo shirt with the collar turned up. He sidled up to me and jokingly introduced himself.

"Welcome to the D.C. office of Progressive Futures. I'm Adam Jacobs. I'll be your regional director while your here." I apologized for my lateness, but he just shrugged. He clearly hadn't been keeping track. We exchanged pleasantries for a couple of minutes before the meeting got started.

I stood in a circle around Adam with the three or four other directors. He told us that he wanted to "roll out the plan of attack for this weekend." We had goals, such as scheduling 15 new canvassers, for Monday. We needed to have three interview sessions every day of the week and build up Saturdays and Sundays. Our staff should average $150 next week, $170 the week after, and $190 the following week. We were to raise $37,000 in the upcoming week. The way to reach these goals, Adam told us, was to "rock out today and tomorrow." He pointed at me and one of the other new directors.

"I want you two to put up 400 posters on the GW campus, that's 200 apiece." Adam ended the meeting and I found myself back out on the street, walking up 20th in the blistering heat. Bobby was walking with me. I had met him at training and I considered him a member of the group of people who asked infuriating amounts of hypothetical questions. But he was ok to talk to, because he loved to talk. He was a native of the D.C. area and he had a lot to tell me about it. There was a long time to tell it, too. We walked past M Street and K Street and we just kept walking until we finally ran into the campus. I was carrying two hundred bright yellow legal-sized posters in my hands and two rolls of tape in the cargo pockets of my shorts. I was covered in sweat, and I found the nearest building and lapped up water out of a water fountain.

Bobby and I spent the next two hours plastering walls and kiosks with the yellow posters. They had photocopied pictures of Barack Obama on them, along with a quote. "Change will not come if we wait for some other person or some other time. We are the ones we've been waiting for," it read. The top of the posters screamed "Campaign Jobs to elect Obama!" and the bottom portion promised $1,400 to $2,200 a month. There were tear-away tags with our office number.

Those posters would become a recurring symbol of my time at Progressive Futures. Again and again, they challenged me to prove how much I wanted victory in this election. At the same time, a serious question developed in my mind as to whether my hanging these posters had any bearing on the election and whether the vagaries on them led people in the right direction. These thoughts came up later, though. At that point, I felt a sense of accomplishment. Bobby and I decided to get back to the office to await further instruction. I asked Adam if it was OK if I got some lunch, and he said it was fine as long as I got back to the office in a half hour. He had a job for me. I went to the Subway across the street and ate as quickly as I could.

The job turned out to be less strenuous than the postering. I was to evaluate the office from an interviewee's perspective. Adam said I brought fresh eyes to the office. I spent the next few hours observing the office and checking out what they had up on the walls. It was two rooms, an office adjoining one, a bathroom another, and a small alcove between the two. The front room of the office was a flurry of activity, even on a Saturday. Two people my age, were there, and they looked furious at having to work on a Saturday. I would have introduced myself, but both were fuming. Every time the phone next to their computers would ring, they would look at each other, glare at me, and grab the phone. I could tell they wanted me to answer the damn thing, but they seemed too sullen to let me in on just how to go about that. It sat on a filing cabinet between a couple of old PCs. There were papers strewn about everywhere in that front room of the office, and the trash bins were overflowing. Among some of the papers, I recognized several forms I had learned about at training. Forms like the travel voucher and payment requisition that I had been taught to fill out and send to Boston with the utmost care sat in random piles all around.

The same was true of the alcove, which was lined with shelves carrying more assorted piles. There were tax forms, contribution forms, interviewee applications everywhere. The back room was more open. There were lots of steel folding chairs leaning against both walls, and most of it was bare carpet. There were a couple of mini-fridges in one corner, and I opened one of them. The stench made me regret it. The male director went through the room on his way to the bathroom a few minutes after I had checked out the place and shouted out,

"It smells like shit in here! Did someone open the fridge?" I owned up to it and he warned me never to do it again. The fridge was only slightly less disgusting than the bathroom. There was no toilet paper dispenser and no toilet paper and no paper towels to dry your hands, just a grimy old towel. The sink and toilet did function, though, and I could tell people used them.

I also noted what was up on the walls. The adornment was a hodgepodge of old candidate yard signs, inspiring quotes, and autographs from random personalities. There was a Dodd for President sign right next to a Hugo Black quote right next to an autograph personalized to DNC canvassers from Terry McCauliffe. The old DNC chairman called our operation "the best program in the history of the DNC." A Howard Dean autograph imploring our canvassers to "keep up the good work" languished elsewhere on a wall. There was a huge map of America with picture cutouts of progressive candidates running for office in all fifty states. Unfortunately, all of the races took place in 2006.

I could tell that people had more important things to do than worry about keeping the office spiffy and up to date. I wanted to know what those things might be, but it would have to wait for another day. Adam didn't seem that interested in what I had to say about the walls and cleanliness of the office, and he began to indicate that it was getting nearer to when we would be leaving. It was eight 'o clock and I had worked my first ten-hour day. I was exhausted. I went back to the house where I was staying and fell asleep without eating dinner.

I came back to the office on Sunday morning. It was my first full day of canvassing. I raised money that day at Dupont Circle with a canvasser named Kaye. She was a great one. Kaye's family had fled the military junta in Myanmar for America, and she was canvassing for Progressive Futures in her summer off from college, where she was a pre-med. She was full of energy and spirit. When people passed by, she would look them in the eye and say "Do you have minute for Democrat? Barack Obama!" Many people didn't know what to make of her. They saw her as a rotund Asian girl accosting them in the street. But many also could see instantly what she was, a young woman doing everything she could for a good cause. That's why people often did what she entreated them to do with all the force of her personality. She raised thousands and thousands of dollars for the DNC. I'll never forget the time she badgered a guy in Georgetown to give \$44 for the 44th president instead of settling for \$20.

"You give forty-four!" she said, smiling but showing she meant it.

"No, I'll just do twenty."

"No, you give forty-four!" The guy laughed at first but then began to threaten not to give at all. Kaye took his \$20, but she raised more money that day than anyone else.

I was lucky to canvass with someone like her on my first day. It was a long, steamy day that Sunday. The seat of my shorts was covered in sweat stains, and people are strange in Dupont. There are factors you need to understand about a neighborhood's people before you can be an effective canvasser there. I was not privy to those of the fashionable Dupont neighborhood on my first day. People there are subjected to canvassers for almost every cause there is almost every day of the week. That's because the people who live there are wealthy, pleasant, and generous. They give money to causes all the time, so they know what spiels are, and the script is the surest thing to turn them off.

Not knowing this, I was out there on my first day reminding people that it was a "defining moment in our nation" and that "Barack Obama is working hand in hand with the DNC." All day, people cut me off. "OK. OK. I know all of this. Are you looking for money?" When I started the day, I would try to avoid their question and stay on the rap. When that turned people off, I just began to admit that I was raising money. And that's when people started giving. After a day of these types of exchanges, I had raised $180. It was a good start, but I knew I had a lot to learn. One woman who interrupted my spiel got under my skin, and it took me a while to recover.

"OK, I don't need to be lectured," she said.

"I'm sorry, Ma'am, I-" she interjected again.

"Look, I've already given money, and I don't need to be lectured. I don't need to be scared. I don't need to be threatened, OK?" And she walked away before I could even respond. It was stunning to have my motives questioned to my face without being given a chance to defend myself. I was standing out in the sun all day working for a cause that both of us believed in, but that woman chose to bear ill will towards me. It was surprising. I expected Republicans to berate me, but I never could have predicted how many times Democrats would hurt my feelings. The toughest part of canvassing is staying positive after people who believe in your cause communicate that they don't believe in you. I didn't know how to do this, and it was several hours before I greeted people with the same energy I used at the start of the day.

I had the same problem the next day in Alexandria. I was standing on King Street in Old Town when I tried to stop a middle-aged white guy in an oxford shirt and khakis. He turned me down, walked past me, and then all of a sudden whirled around.

"You guys are here every day," he said.

"Well, yes, sir, I know we are but—"

"It's getting annoying. You guys hassle me every day and I'm tired of it."

Now, I didn't know whether this man was a Republican or not, but it didn't matter. He left an impression. Out on the cobblestones of Old Town in the mid-July sun, I wondered if I liked what I was doing. I didn't know if it was worthwhile.

It took an hour or so of quiet mutterings at passersby before I realized that that guy wasn't worth my thought. I knew then that I will stop and encourage every canvasser I meet for the rest of my life. I'll give money if I can, but at the very least, I'll tell them I like what they're doing. I believe that canvassing is a civic discussion. Kansas City was an infuriating place to be for me sometimes when I was growing up because nobody seemed to want to talk about anything. Sure, you can talk about the weather, or the Chiefs, or a television show, but try to probe a social issue and you will find a reluctance bordering on coldness.

This Midwestern dryness is a means of maintaining the status quo. It benefits the powerful parties who like keeping their power, and it keeps people from working together for a greater good. If people examined issues in public more, intellectual arguments would win the day out in the open, where rationality rules. I needed to urge people to participate in a discussion for a couple of minutes instead of being passive participants in civic life. I figured that the middle and upper classes would vote Republican if they worried about their finances, but that they would vote Democrat if they believed that this election was a defining moment. At this point, nobody would have believed that Americans would vote Democrat both because they were worried about their finances and because they thought this election was a chance to set the country on a better path.

I had to remind myself why I liked what I was doing in Alexandria, and I finally turned my day around. I imagined people walking down King Street were old acquaintances from Missourah who wanted to stay in their Republican shells. This was my chance to wake them up. I relished the opportunity.

Chapter 6

From In Explanation of Our Times

The folks with no titles in front of their names
all over the world
are raring up and talking back
to the folks called Mister.

-Langston Hughes

I decided I wanted to stay in D.C. while I was I was riding the train across the Potomac for the night.

The Metrorail system is D.C. It is the District's demeanor, its moods, its desires. It was 10 p.m. on July 22, and the train was packed. The men wore suits and ties and exhausted expressions. The women lugged their purses and cloth grocery bags full of necessities. It was obvious that these people had put in just as long a workday as I had.

D.C. is a town of workaholics. There's a sense that the one who labors for a cause day and night will see it come to fruition, while the one who relaxes will lose. The Metro is full of people working hard for what they believe in, or people working hard to make ends meet, or people working hard to try to find a way to make ends meet. They're on the Metro every day.

When you ride the Metro and smell the heat coming up from the tracks and you maneuver for position in crowds, you begin to see what it takes to succeed here. If the door to a train is still open, you'd better run for that opening, or you'd better stay out of the way of people who want to run. You need to stay to the right if you don't want to walk up the escalators, or you need to walk up them quickly because you might be late. You need to know the color and endpoint of the line where you need to make your transfer, or you'll miss it. You need to be willing to stand in big crowds during rush hour, to be an individual akin to a worker bee in the hive. And you need to be comfortable with people who come from places as diverse as Ohio and Anacostia, Belarus and Africa. You need to decide if you are going to stand up or sit next to a stranger.

I was standing up on a yellow line train headed for Huntington that night, but it wasn't because I was uncomfortable sitting next to anyone. The car was jammed. It was as if I had found a second rush hour of people who had been in the office until 10 p.m. I was gripping one of the rods hanging down from the ceiling, and I kept swinging from side to side when the car would stop and start. I took in the people on that car. I saw that they had come to the Capitol to make an impact. And I saw that it would take a lot to convince one of these people to give me money on the street. I saw that I would have to learn to talk and move faster and smarter than I ever had in Missourah. I knew then, hurtling over the Potomac, that I wanted to be one of these people.

I was on a high. I had spent the day canvassing on the sunny bricks of a Starbucks in Silver Spring. It was the kind of experience that canvassers know as a "party in the street." The term is an accurate reflection of the elation that comes with smiling all day at strangers and feeling them smiling back. It's a time when a canvasser earns rapport with everyone he or she speaks with on first impression. I only raised $131 that day, but it was the first time I felt that great feeling, and it would be far from the last.

A couple of interactions stood out for me that day. An attractive middle-aged black woman with cropped gray hair gave me a $20 bill. She had seemed unsure at first, but I convinced her that this election could be different if Democrats worked harder this year than we ever have. Due to campaign finance law, all of the donors are required to disclose their occupations, and we shared a moment when I told her that my parents were both teachers like her. She said to me, "Well, your parents sure raised you well." I grinned and thanked her.

And I remember a gorgeous lawyer who almost passed me by. When I asked her whether she had a minute for the Democrats, she gave a standard response, saying, "I'm already a Democrat." I shot back, "Great, you're exactly who I need to talk to." She stopped in her tracks. Less than a minute later, she was making out a $50 check to the DNC. When she was putting her billfold back together, an assortment of coins spilled out all over the ground. You better believe I was on my hands and knees grabbing every single one of them. I would do that for every one of my donors because I loved every one of them for believing in me and believing in Barack Obama. And if getting on my hands and knees to beg were the best way to raise money, I would have been on my hands and knees begging for Barack Obama and begging these people to love me enough to support him.

I realized that I had to do everything I could to become a great canvasser. The stakes were too high in this election and canvassing was too big a challenge to back down. I would need to will contributions by sheer energy. I had begun to notice that there were people who could have contributed at lot but only contributed a little. I wasn't communicating the urgency that I needed to when a housewife reached into her Coach bag and handed me a couple of singles. I had a feeling that I was letting people off the hook, that people saw me as a nice boy but not necessarily the kind of person who could seal the deal. I've been fighting that impression my whole life, and the aching that it has caused to my temperament motivates me to beat it every day.

One time that day, two ladies walked past me in conversation. I interrupted them and asked them loudly if they had a minute for the Democrats. They waved at me and told me they were already

Democrats. Not missing a beat, I said they were exactly who I should talk to. They didn't stop, but they laughed and one said to the other, "Damn, he's got balls." That was the highlight of my day.

I realized that I would need to be loud. I would need to be a little obnoxious. I would have to be a salesman with a response ready at all times, possibly one including a rhyme. The more ridiculous I was, the more people could see how much I wanted it. It was strange, but I felt I could build the best rapport with people by being crazy. As I lay in bed at night, phrases I could use with people when they gave such and such response bounced around my head. It was difficult to fall asleep with that din and difficult to fall asleep when I wanted it to be tomorrow already.

I was staying in a tony neighborhood of south Arlington, and my circumstances could not have been better. The friends who hosted me were career government employees who had a vacant basement. I made myself comfortable in a bedroom, a living room and a bathroom. As if that weren't enough, they provided me with their great company. Stan and Jenny already had treated me to several home-cooked meals. They mixed their food with a keen understanding of the way Washington and the country functioned. Stan said he supported Obama because he had spent so little time in the Senate. As far as he was concerned, the smaller the tenure in that institution, the better.

"I've lived here for thirty years," he told me. "And they've never done anything."

I laughed and Stan repeated himself, slapping his hand on the counter.

"Nothing! Thirty years and nothing!"

"OK, darlin'," Jenny cut in. "We know."

Stan looked back at me.

"Thirty years!" he exclaimed in a hushed voice.

"Darlin!" Jenny said. I lucked into this one. I had a living space, food, and great hosts. None of these is a traditional aspect of employment at Progressive Futures. The company had no concern for the living quarters of its employees. My own story showed that they would send you anywhere at any time if you let them. I wanted to be on the front lines of this election, but I didn't want to be dropped in a random small town in a random swing state with nowhere to stay but a random couch. Besides, nothing could be more front and center than the nation's capital.

I got a call from Eddie Kliensasser one night. He was still in Austin, and he was just about to go down to Sixth Street.

"Don't you have a job?" I asked him.

"Nope."

"Are you in the process of finding one?"

"Nope."

"So what have you been doing?"

"Oh you know, same old, same old. I've been boozing, partying, smoking. Most people are still in town. It's a lot of fun."

"Oh, I'm sure it is. Some people have to work for a living, though. Does anyone have a job?"

"Oh yea, we made one of the pledges get a job flipping burgers at Dirty Martin's so he could get us cheap beer."

I was starting to get angry. "Haven't you guys graduated? And I thought it was summer. Are there pledge classes in the summer now?"

"Yeah, we graduated, but this guy just keeps listening to us so he can hang out with us. It's pretty pathetic, really. Anyways, how's D.C.?" I told him how hard I was working, how I was learning to get people to donate right on the spot, and how I almost didn't have enough to live on in my bank account.

"That's a bummer, man," Eddie said. "But I've got some good news for you. I'm coming to D.C."

"What? When?" I had no idea he was even thinking of moving to DC.

"I'm moving up there at the end of this month. My aunt owns a house in Glover Park that she rents out, and there's a vacancy, so I'm coming. She's been up there a long time, and she's well-connected, so I'm thinking she can find me a job, too. Are you going to be there? You said something about being moved somewhere else, so I didn't know if you were still in D.C."

"Well, yeah," I said. "They want me to work on this other campaign in a swing state or something, but now I don't know if I want to do that."

"Well, you better not, man. I'm coming up, so you better not do something dumb and move somewhere else. This stuff you're doing sounds intense, so you're gonna need to let loose on occasion. I can usually help with that."

I agreed, and told him that I would stay in D.C. We hung up a little while later when Eddie figured he'd better get moving toward Sixth Street.

I went on the record in a directors meeting the following day. When all the tasks for the day were finished, Ellen Newman liked to call meetings. We would pull up the ratty swivel chairs and the steel folding chairs around her. Ellen was our canvass director. She was my direct supervisor and the manager of our office, a tall brunette with a motherly bearing and a sweet personality.

When all of us talked that night, a couple of the other directors expressed their frustration at not being placed in a voter registration office yet. Ellen looked at them with firm and serious eyes and told them that situations like these weren't unusual at Progressive Futures. When it was my turn, I let her know that I wanted to stay in her office. Tears welled up in her eyes. It felt good to be wanted and it made me feel secure that I made the right choice.

The following day, Ellen gave me a full day's lesson in canvassing. We went to the Shirlington neighborhood of Arlington, and the instruction began well before we reached the site. As we waited for the bus at the Pentagon Metro station, she drilled me on the rap, asking me to repeat it again and again. Then she had me practice responding to the typical excuses for not giving: the person had already given or would rather give online. In both circumstances, Ellen preached what we called the "response structure." Progressive Futures advocated using this technique every time someone didn't want to give after the initial script. After the person turned us down, we were supposed to ask,

"Are you with us on this campaign?" The person would answer yes, of course, that's why I stopped in the street in the middle of my busy day, or any variation on those themes. It's a patronizing question to which the canvasser already knows the answer. But once the person acknowledges support, the canvasser can create another avenue for asking the person to donate. This is called "retargeting," and it occurs when the canvasser confronts the person with a new appeal. My go-to argument during this time involved the idea of getting people personally invested in this election. I would tell them that we all realized how much work we would need to do to take down the Republicans. It required a massive amount of civic participation on our parts. When you give to me, you are not only buying into the Democratic ground game that can deliver this election for Democrats everywhere. You're also starting a conversation tree that can spread around the nation. You can always talk to your friends about politics, and I wouldn't make the claim that the only way to get involved is by donating. But when you give to the party, you are making an investment that will motivate you and all Democrats to pull through all the way to November. The way Democrats can win this election against the powerful interests that support Republicans is by standing up together like never before, and that's why I'm asking you to give today.

It was compelling, and I had used it and refined it throughout the week. Ellen gave it her blessing, and she stood by me in the traditional "face-to-face" setup on the sidewalk outside the shops in Shirlington. This arrangement means two canvassers facing each other and speaking only to passersby coming toward them. It was the setup we used most often. On that outing, it was useful because it allowed Ellen to give me pointers all day.

"Grab them from further away," she said when I couldn't stop some group because they were nearly past me when I began talking to them.

"I think you missed a contributor there," she told me when I let a woman get away. "It's always good to ask for $270 for the number of electoral votes Obama needs, but make sure people know they don't have to give that much."

I won my first contribution from a woman who was not an American citizen. I asked if she had a minute for the Democrats from about twenty feet away, and she told me that she wasn't yet a citizen. I responded that if she were a legal permanent resident, she could get her voice into this historic election. That made her stop. I gave a great rap, but she said she didn't have any cash on her. So I used the response structure and my compelling argument. I also reminded her that we took all forms of payment. She contributed $25 by credit card. Noncitizens were solid contributors the entire election season. Legal permanent residents are entitled by law to make campaign donations, and I made the pitch again and again that this would allow a legal permanent resident to throw his or her support to Barack Obama and the Democrats. When I started, I felt strange about discussing a person's citizenship status in public, but the longer I canvassed the more comfortable I became with it. Everything about canvassing is awkward, so it fit right in. During the course of my work in this election, I would say that more than half of the legal permanent residents I spoke to ended up making some kind of a donation. It was a remarkable ratio not attributable to my skills as a canvasser, but rather to the extent that Barack Obama inspired people from all walks of life. And when legal permanent residents who have made contributions to the Democrats become citizens, they will become permanent Democrats.

My next contributor that day was a college student I convinced to donate all of the cash in her wallet. She was not interested at first, but my argument brought her around. I made the claim that the party would be more responsible and accountable to young people like her and me if she could support me in my effort to build up small donations. As you know, I told her, we aren't taking any contributions from special interest PACs and corporate lobbyists. If we win the election by raising the money in small chunks, it will mean that the party is no longer beholden to people who could put down $28,500 at the drop of a hat. The entire electoral landscape would change. She had only $16 in her wallet, but it was a rush nonetheless.

My adrenaline had been activated. Every time someone gave, it would give me a little more confidence and a little more energy. Each succeeding passerby would see a broader smile and hear me a bit sooner than they would have before. I still hadn't received a $100 donation, and I was on the prowl. Ellen said I had the skills to bring one in, that it would come, that I shouldn't get hung up on it. I couldn't relax, though. I wouldn't feel confident in my ability until I had achieved that first $100 contribution.

Late in the afternoon, a well-dressed middle-aged woman came by. She told me she was a small business owner, and the Democrats might raise her taxes, but she was so fed up with Bush that she had to vote our way. She reminded me of my old boss from high school, the one who employed me to scoop frozen custard and took me to Royals games. I gave her my civic participation argument. I could tell she was buying into it. Like everyone who wanted to hear what I had to say, she was captivated. She wasn't checking her watch or cutting me off because she thought she knew better. She was standing still and letting my appeal sink in. Any competent canvasser could predict what happened next. She reached for her checkbook and donated $100.

That day in Shirlington was a powerful lesson in canvassing. I had a goal in mind and I achieved it, but it had taken all day. I needed those first two small donations to give me the confidence to get the larger one later in the day. I also learned that I didn't need to be crazy to win support every day. I had used the voice of a pragmatic salesman with all sirs and m'ams and clever turns of phrase. I was a polite young man who convinced people. For the rest of the summer and fall, I shifted between those two personalities when I was canvassing, sometimes being one or the other, sometimes being a combination. My pragmatic salesman could begin to sound arrogant, scripted, and overly clever, so I had to dial him down and stick to the rap. My crazy man could become too intense for someone just walking to lunch, so I had to lay off it a bit and talk a little more slowly. Every successful canvasser has a personal style, and these were mine. I could change from one to the other at the drop of a hat.

What never would have raised money is revealing how desperate I was for these donations. It was no longer just an idea that I was raising a little money for a good cause, or even a lot of money for the defining moment in our nation. My daily totals were a referendum on my personal ability. I was looking for affirmation in the real world. Sure, I could sit in a classroom and make A's and all my teachers would give me compliments, but this was a challenge. If I couldn't get people to give me money on the street, I would be an ineffective political operative and an unsuccessful person. The Democrats would lose and I would be just a nice boy who couldn't make it outside the classroom. I drew the lines in my head that way every day, and I lived for the rush. But if this sense of anxiety had invaded my raps, I would have turned people away the way any strange person who shows an unseemly attachment toward some single goal or purpose does. I disguised myself with smiles and jokes and had a great time of it.

On our way back to the Metro, a couple of guys in a patio restaurant stopped us as we walked by. They turned out to be from the DCCC, and they encouraged us, telling us how important what we were doing was and to stick with it. They wanted to know where we had grown up, where we went to college, how long we had been working.

"Well, Ima just a humble boy from Missourah," I said, swinging my arms back and forth in a gesture of down-home simplicity. "I come to the big city to learn me some politic." Everyone laughed and one of the guys looked at Ellen and asked,

"Is he always like this?" She nodded.

Chapter 7

From The Waking

I wake to sleep, and take my waking slow.
I feel my fate in what I cannot fear.
I learn by going where I have to go.

-Theodore Roethke

 A checkout lady at the Harris Teeter validated my labors. It was 11 on a weeknight, and I was buying groceries because I was tired of mooching off Stan and Jenny. The woman behind the counter was old and overweight and ready to go. She was waiting on another employee to take her spot for the night.
 I said I hoped I wasn't keeping her late, and she could tell I meant it. She motioned for me to put the few groceries I was buying on the conveyor belt.
 "What you do so late that you gotta get groceries right now?" She asked. I told her. She stopped running my items over the pricing machine for a split and looked over at me.
 "That's important work." It was as affirming a compliment as I have ever received. When I unloaded the groceries from my car, I stared for a second at the moon and vowed that I was doing this for her.
 It's my contention that working people in America need to stick together more. I'm talking about the middle-class people

who have steady jobs and comfortable incomes, but I'm also talking about the people who work two and three jobs to make ends meet and live paycheck to paycheck. Barack Obama is the kind of figure that both groups can support. He inspires middle-class people as much as he promises a helping had for the poor. Depending on whether he realizes his potential, Obama could create a coalition for the Democrats that will provide a basis for longstanding expansion of liberal social programs. If I could stand in a grocery checkout lane as a middle-class white boy and connect with an old black woman, our two groups could vote our common interests against the elites. Four decades of politics had weakened the Great Society, but this was our chance to get it back.

I canvassed every day with these thoughts ringing in my head. I demanded constant effort of myself, and I gave every conversation of every hour of every day my best. I never thought of it as anything else than my chance to make an imprint on the election, and I measured my impact by the dollar.

Such grandiose notions fed my hunger to become a better canvasser. I started tasting regular success. News added to the arguments I used. A July 27 article in *The Washington Post* reported that John McCain had raised $1.1 million from oil company executives after he reversed his position on offshore drilling. I thought it was a notable coincidence that the D.C. office of Progressive Futures made the same amount of money its goal for the summer. I wanted to impart to people that Obama and the Dems could raise the same amount of money as big oil using many small donations from people like you and me. I thought it was brilliant. Everything changed a week or so later when Obama shifted course and took roughly the same position as McCain, but that story was my bread and butter while it lasted.

And it worked. I saw people transformed during the course of the discussion. An Ethiopian woman with a heavy accent began a conversation with me outside a Starbucks on 14th and P by indicating that she was aware of how legal permanent residents could register their voices in this election, and that she had already given. She was stepping away to go into Starbucks, so I needed to say something fast. I shelved the regular rap and went into my argument about how thousands of small donors could beat the fat cats by giving in small amounts and mobilizing each other to the polls. A guy she was with went inside to get whatever drinks they wanted, while she stood and listened. I knew I had her. A few minutes later, her boyfriend returned to find her writing a $50 check. He was livid and argued with her in their native tongue. I just stood with my hands clasped together and a warm smile on my face like a learned student of Master Confucius who has grasped the rituals of society.

I had a similar interaction with a middle-aged man outside the Starbucks by Dupont Circle the following day. When I asked him if he had a minute for the Democrats, he answered, "Yes, but I won't give you any money." I again dropped the standard script and went into my argument. The man's features softened and he listened patiently to my reasoning. Resigned, he forked over a $10 bill. It's exhilarating to change a mind in a minute.

Canvassers need to be able to do this in the well-heeled Dupont area. As I have noted before, it's a remarkable place to canvass. All day on my first Saturday canvassing there, people asked me right off if I wanted money. All week, I had sidestepped the question and launched into the rap, the approach that works in places where people need to be inspired to give for the first time. That day, I went back to the technique I learned on my first day canvassing in Dupont. I answered yes to every one of them. I would say, "Here's why." Then my argument would pour out like water out of a faucet. My brain became so accustomed to saying it that I could read whether people were buying it as I talked. They did that day. I raised $353, my biggest total so far. One guy had a foot inside the door of a store while he was telling me that he makes regular contributions. "That's great," I said, "We can get your next one out of the way." He gave $50.

I could see that trading your mother's milk for gall was a necessity in this business. The following Monday, I canvassed outside Union Station with the highest grossing canvasser on our staff, a rabbi's son by the name of Avi. I had a rough time that day. It was nice to exercise my right to badger people on the street in the shadow of the Capitol, but few people paid me any mind. "I already work for the Democrats," people would say with an air of resentment as they passed me by. After a couple of hours, I was muttering feebly, hoping not to offend. I called Avi over and asked him if I could watch him canvass for a few minutes. I was amazed by what I saw. The passersby near Union Station were packs of busy working people, but almost every one of them responded to Avi. He smiled and waved at all of them, clearly addressing the person he was speaking to. It was not the "Excuse me, sir" that I would say when a guy was a few steps away, it was "Hi sir!" in a firm voice directed toward the person twenty feet away. He didn't care about looking strange to people who walked by. He didn't care what they thought. He was here to do a job, and this was the best way to do it.

"Your raps are good," Avi said. "But you'll get more contributions when you get more stops. It's all about the stops." He was right, but it took several weeks before I understood how to do what he did.

I was learning, though, and it felt good. I can remember standing near the Dupont Metro entrance on that Saturday I had spent canvassing in Dupont. I had just completed my first full week in the office, and I was listening to a brass band that used to set up on the sidewalk on summer nights. Sweating black men in white undershirts were playing trumpets and tubas and trombones. A circle of people had gathered around, and there were children dancing. As the players powered through their melody again and again, people left to hit the bars and couples walked away to go have dinner. I was exhausted from canvassing seven days in a row, but I lingered until they couldn't play any more.

I was becoming acquainted with the color of the Dupont area. One of the times I was canvassing there, there was a man wearing ten Obama buttons on various parts of his dress shirt, apparently going to his office as an Obama billboard. He saw me laughing as he walked towards me.

"What?" he said. "What are you going to ask me? Are you going to ask me if I'm a Democrat or if I support Obama?" He introduced himself as Lance, and he told me how he had become such a huge fan of Obama that he walked around with at least ten buttons on at all times and talked about him all day to anyone who would listen. Then he pulled out a big plastic bag full of Obama buttons and offered me my pick.

"But only take one," he said. "These have to last." He put them away and said he was going into Starbucks.

"Do you want anything? And oh, by the way, here's my credit card. Put fifty bucks on it, and not a penny more, do you understand?" I said yes, I understood, and I made out a contributor form for $50 while he got me an iced coffee.

For some reason, when he came back, I remembered that I wanted to ask a local the best place to get a haircut. Something told me Lance would know the right place.

"Oh yes, there are plenty of good places to go in Dupont," he said. "Just look for any place that has a rainbow sticker. But if you want the best one, go see Donnell at VSL Hair Design, the place right next to that Subway on Connecticut. Where are you from?" I told him I was from Missourah.

"Oh yes, you need to go see Donnell at VSL. It will be quite an experience for you." He was right. I went to VSL later that day, and the guy at the front desk there quoted me for a haircut at $30, which was the same price I paid in Austin. I made an appointment with Donnell for the following day.

Donnell was a heavyset black man wearing jeans and a shaded golf hat. I was sitting on a bench enjoying the bouncy techno music VSL had playing when he walked up and introduced himself.

"Let's bring you back here, young man," he said. "Follow me." He sat me in his chair and looked me over.

"My goodness! You are a hairy, hairy man! How long has it been since you got a haircut?" A month, I said.

"A month? And that's how your neck looks? You need to come in here on a regular schedule, hairy as you are. Go over there and get your shampoo." He motioned to the line of chairs set up next to sinks. "Alfredo, can you shampoo my client?"

A muscular man in a skin-tight shirt set my head inside the washing sink and wet my hair. When he put the shampoo on, it was like a massage on the top of my head, complete with rubbing and fingernails. He worked his hands around to my ears and washed behind them tenderly.

"That feels good, huh?" Alfredo said. I nodded. He applied the conditioner in the same way and dried off my hair before sending me back to Donnell.

"Alright, young man," Donnell said. "You have pretty short hair, so this should be easy to do. I'm just going to add some texture to it, and you'll be out of here in no time looking great." He began to work on my hair, asking a lot of questions while doing so. He said I had made the right decision in coming to D.C.

"You've come to the right place. There are a lot of straight bitches here, and, young as you are, you should fuck your brains out. Do you have a girlfriend?" No, I said.

"Oh, well, then you especially need to play the field." He said it as if having a girlfriend would mean that I would need to 'play the field' to a lesser extent. I was laughing and comfortable, and I wanted to see how Donnell would react, so I told him I was a virgin.

"Oh, Jesus, that's the stupidest thing I've ever heard. Alfredo, did you hear that? We've got a virgin over here. How old are you?" Twenty-three, I said.

"A twenty-three year-old virgin! You must have no game at all. Well, don't worry, stick with me here, and you'll get laid in no time." I laughed, but I had no idea that he would be right. And I kept seeing Donnell every month because laughing at yourself while getting a professional haircut is cheaper and more edifying than going to a shrink.

I didn't see Lance again until the week before the election, when I was canvassing at 17th and R. I didn't recognize him because he wasn't wearing his buttons.

"Don't you remember me?" he asked. "I gave you fifty bucks and a Starbucks." Then I remembered him. I asked where his buttons were.

"I gave them away. I do this every election. I get hyped up about another Democrat, and I go crazy and tell people how great the Democrats are and give a thousand bucks to them, and then I see that he's not even going to support me getting married to the person I love. All the Democrats do is ask for my money around election time, but when push comes to shove, they won't stand up to the religious right. I'm sick of it, that's all."

I didn't respond with any rap or try to convince him otherwise because I knew Lance was right.

The following Sunday morning was the first time in ten days I could sleep in. It felt so good that I had to take the entire day off. I was told to plaster the American University campus with 200 "Campaign jobs to elect Obama!" posters, but it didn't happen. I did go over to the AU campus. It was raining and the campus looked muddy, uncollegiate, and locked. I tossed the posters in the trash and split. The posters were not important to me. I couldn't link laboring for two hours taping these posters up with Barack Obama winning the election. And I didn't feel like finding that connection on a rainy Sunday afternoon. I still was surprised I threw the damn things away. I had vowed to do everything I could. The guilt mechanisms of my brain activated themselves with the thought of McCain staffers not taking a day off. If the other side outworked us, they would win.

That thought was another paranoid creation of the guilt mechanisms of my brain. For one, McCain's ground game was old or nonexistent. They never even began to put posters up for canvassing jobs until the last weeks of the election when Florida began to be in doubt. For another, I realized that it was pure arrogance to pretend that I would be the reason Barack Obama won, if he did. I did realize that forces beyond my control would decide the election. The issues, the gaffes, the news would determine the winner, not a guy badgering people on the street. And our side wouldn't win automatically if there were more bodies badgering people in the street for money. Progressive Futures, Inc. had its own stake in this election, and that was to make money. At that time, I didn't grasp how its contract with the DNC worked. I also didn't know for sure whether PFI was a for-profit corporation. I knew that these two questions were what Donald Rumsfeld called known unknowns. Progressive Futures had interests in this election that were not my interests, and they may have been interests separate from those of the Democrats. Even if Howard Dean and Vern Phillips had the same interests, they were different people with different employers. To act as if everything that I did for Progressive Futures was unequivocal in either its goodness or utility would have been deceiving myself. Fortunately, I didn't act that way. Instead. I bought an ice cream cone from Maggie Moo's.

My hosts Stan and Jenny loved that story. They had counseled me that what PFI was doing to me was probably illegal, and they always enjoyed hearing any small defiance I could make against PFI staff policies. They cooked me dinner that night and had more interesting things to say. They told me about Myers-Briggs typology, which classifies people according to psychiatric personality tests based on Jungian models. Jenny recommended taking a test. She said she thought she was crazy until this test showed her that she was a certain kind of person.

I knew exactly what she meant, so I took a couple of short tests online. My answers to fifty or sixty questions called me an INFJ, which classifies my personality as having the traits of introverted, intuition, feeling and, my strongest trait, judgmental. My type made me what the site referred to as a "Counselor Idealist," who feels deep compassion for loved ones, possesses writing skills, and leads by example. According to these sites, only 1 to 3 percent of people fall under this category, the rarest type. I'd like to take a real test in a laboratory with a control group, but I liked the online test results.

The results had a cautionary note, too. The upside of my strong judgmental trait is that I can understand others' perspectives and that's the downside too. The test warned never to express anger because what I said to others might be extremely hurtful. This warning squared with my experience. I've never gotten in any shouting matches in my life because I don't have a pugnacious bone in my body. But I can feel sorry for myself, and when I do, I have a tendency to try to make other people feel sorry for me. And it usually works. Someday I hope I will conquer this self-pity. On that day, I will have learned to find the most affirming things to say to everyone I meet. And I hope I'll have the strength to say them.

That reflective day off helped me a lot. Nobody at the office asked me about the posters and I needed to salvage what days of rest I could get. I worked twelve hours the day when I went to Union Station and fifteen the next. I couldn't believe what I had done when I completed those fifteen hours. It was not routine to work from 8:30 a.m. to 11 p.m, but it was expected of the director who stayed for the night crew. I hadn't been aware of this night crew, but it was the same thing as our day crew, only it worked from 1 to 9 instead of 9 to 5. This smaller band of canvassers existed but I hadn't known about it. I did on that Tuesday night, though. I was in front of the computer processing the numbers for the day for the day well after the other street directors had left. My blue DNC shirt was caked with my sweat from the day, and I couldn't figure out all the spreadsheets I had to fill out to report our numbers to the national office. Plus, the phone was ringing off the hook and I had barely eaten. I had never worked this hard in my life.

My bank account had nothing to show for it. There was $9 in checking and $7 in savings and it began to feel like a punch in the stomach. When you have no money, you feel as if you can't go inside anywhere in a city like D.C. A proper meal was too expensive, so restaurants were off limits. A cold beer costs a ludicrous sum, so the bars were closed to me. Even a cold drink during my swamp-ass canvassing day would throw me beyond my means. I could afford to spend no more than $10 a day, and that would usually end up being lunch.

I was exhausted and hungry that night when I grabbed the last Metro of the night back out to Arlington. While commuting, I ran into an old classmate from Texas who was in DC working for a Pro-Israel lobbying group, and she had distressing news. Most people in her organization were supporting McCain. She said they thought he would be a better ally of Israel and that some of them wondered whether Obama was a Muslim. It depressed us both. She had been in class with me the last semester of college, and she sported her Obama for President shirt all the time during that long primary season.

There is a split in the Jewish community on Israel that most people either don't know about or don't understand. I'm saying this without any research to back me up, but I am a Jew who has known Jews. It's true that most of us do believe that the state of Israel should be preserved. It's also true that most of us support Israel in any conflict. But it's not true that either of these positions entails approval of every action by the government of Israel or the idea that Israel's interests supersede any other political interests. There are many Jews, like myself, who see the Middle East as less important than ensuring adequate health care for all Americans and who would compromise with Palestinians to end the killing in that conflict. I believe I represent a growing number of liberal Jews who feel this way. I also believe that most of the Pro-Israel lobby is squarely against us. And when my old friend told me this about her bosses, I found one more chip on my shoulder. Any liberal Jew feels the same way about Joe Lieberman as any liberal black does about Clarence Thomas. I had this feeling that "Loserman" would try to mobilize my community against Obama, and I fought him on the streets of D.C. every day.

I talked to Eddie on my cell phone as I walked back to Stan and Jenny's after midnight. He was almost packed. But he didn't have much time to talk, he told me. He was about to go smoke and watch *The Sopranos*. And I was spent and needing to go to sleep to get up the next day and do everything I could to elect Democrats once again. I didn't envy him.

Chapter 8

From When the Frost is on the Punkin

When the frost is on the punkin and the fodder's in the shock,
And you hear the kyouck and gobble of the struttin' turkey cock,
And the clackin' of the guineys, and the cluckin' of the hens,
And the rooster's hallylooyer as he tiptoes on the fence;
O, it's then the time a feller is a-feelin' at his best,
With the risin' sun to greet him from a night of peaceful rest,
As he leaves the house, bareheaded, and goes out to feed the stock,
When the frost is on the punkin and the fodder's in the shock.

-James Whitcomb Riley

The irregularity of my work hours necessitated regularity in my time off. There were few hours when I wasn't working, but I took comfort in a routine. My rituals were constant and meditative.

Whether I got back to Stan and Jenny's at 9, 10, or 11, my first priority was beer. I had to have my Yuengling Black and Tan. Then I would eat a pastrami sandwich, a bowl of granola or grape nuts, and a few frozen grapes while I read the *Post*. You don't know what you're talking about in Washington unless you read that paper.

Dinner complete, I would step quietly downstairs and out a back door to smoke pot. If the stress of Progressive Futures, Inc. hadn't left me when I ate quietly, it left me now. Pot's a reality kick. It makes me detach myself from insignificant matters, sets off pleasant voices in my head, and makes me giggle.

A shower followed. Any good Jewish boy knows that you do not go to sleep in your sweat. That would be an invitation to sickness, which means missing work, which means a trip to the doctor, which means a trip to the drug store, which means an outlay of time and money that wouldn't have been necessary if you had just showered before you went to bed. I was bathing in sweat all day anyways from standing out in the sun and badgering people for money. So I showered.

And of course, I was exhausted, so I just would collapse into bed and read a few lines of poetry. I was reading Sandburg, and his words filled me with thoughts of the greatness of the common man and what he has the potential to accomplish.

But as I lay down, my thoughts would move back to the office. The hundreds of interactions of my day would swirl around in my head. When you spend that much time at the office, you never leave. And I would fall asleep because life is work and tomorrow was another day.

I got up at 6:30 a.m. every day. Stan drove into the District each morning at 7 a.m. to beat the traffic, and I had to be ready. He would drop me at the Judiciary Square metro station, a five-minute ride to Dupont Circle. Stan saved me 45 minutes every morning he did this for me. And just before he dropped me, every day he would point out a squat black newspaper guy who sold papers to cars and passersby. The guy was out there every time, and Stan noticed something different about him each day.

"Look, he's wearing sunglasses this morning," he would say, or "Look, he's got cutoff jeans on today," or, one time, "Look, he's relieving himself over there in the bushes." It was remarkable that Stan could find something different about him every day or that the guy could have something different about him worth commenting upon every day.

The time Stan's ride saved me was precious. I arrived at Dupont Circle at 7:30 or so, earlier than anyone else every day. With no desire to spend any unnecessary time in the office, I brought whatever book I was reading with me. I would park myself on a bench in the median at 20th and Q. The summer mornings were pleasant and I would take up my book and watch the commuters pass and nod at the homeless people who sat on the other benches and smoked cigarettes.

I was reading Hunter S. Thompson's *Fear and Loathing on the Campaign Trail '72*. The political analysis and the anecdotes were amusing and insightful, but I couldn't help thinking Dr. Thompson had it easy. His accommodations were provided for, he had access to the candidates and their staff, and he got to write for *Rolling Stone*. Even those people in Iowa and New Hampshire who get to eat pancakes with every candidate of both parties don't get privileges like that.

At about 8:15 or 8:30, somebody else, usually Ellen, would come walking up to open up the office for the day. We set the tables and chairs against the wall to clear the rooms for everyone. That's when the first observers would begin to arrive. Observers-in- training, or OT's as we called them were people who had interviewed with us and had been invited back for a second interview, an "observation day." In practice, though, it was their first day of work. PFI had been for classifying the "observation day" this way so that the company did not have to pay the interviewee for his or her time, but OT's were now compensated in the same way as our regular employees. The OT system did make sense as a method for hiring, though. Our "interviews" were not highly evaluative and seldom lasted longer than five to ten minutes. You can't tell whether someone will be an effective canvasser in five or ten minutes. A perspective canvasser had to go out in the heat with the snubbing and the forty or fifty repetitions of the rap before he or she could be hired.

This process of turning interviewees to employees was the OT process, and I specialized in it in my first months at Progressive Futures. Every director had "realms," aspects of running the office that they would handle directly, and mine was staff development. I dealt with the OT's every morning. The first step was getting their tax forms, their W-4's and I-9's. Both needed to be filed before they started working. I got this step out of the way right when each OT arrived, so that I wasn't mixing up papers. After I took each person's tax forms, I asked him or her to have a seat and study the rap.

I wanted to help them by giving them something to do. Many were nervous, and they could hover around if you didn't give clear instructions. I don't blame them. Our office was a strange place. Most people didn't even know what to say when I would answer the buzzer downstairs, just like I hadn't on my first day. Then they had to climb up our three flights of stairs and announce themselves where people were already stressed and flying around the office like food service employees during a busy lunchtime. The tax forms and the seat and the rap set them at ease.

The OT's usually numbered about four or five, and they would be seated in the front room of the office as regular employees filtered in. By the time nine o' clock rolled around, the back room was full of the twenty or thirty regular canvassers who had shown up for work that day. I led the OT's into the back room for announcements.

That was one of my favorite times of the day. I asked for and received the privilege of addressing the staff every morning, and I loved it. I always did like a captive audience and the sound of my voice, so I hammed it up. I would start with a round of introductions in which I would ask everyone to state his or her name, his or her hometown, and his or her answer to a question I came up with every day. It was the question of the day portion of the announcements. I asked people to name their favorite Motown artists or their favorite condiment or a song they knew every word to or their favorite comedian or anything I could think of. I would start with me, calling myself "Tobias from Missourah." Then everyone would introduce his or herself and give funny answers. Sometimes the poor OT's would misunderstand the inanity of the exercise and share too much information. There was an old guy one time who introduced himself as a veteran of the Korean War and the shock hung over the room for a split second of silence.

Once everyone had shared, I proceeded with the other announcements. These would fluctuate based on what materials I had, what instructions Ellen gave me, or whatever popped into my head. I would often provide a news update, in which I would talk about the latest campaign developments and instruct people how they could use them in their canvassing. I shared the story I read in the *Post* about McCain getting $1.1 million from oil execs, for example. As the campaign proceeded and the poll numbers began to dictate the mood, these news announcements became more and more necessary to give everyone a picture to draw for people in order to make Democrats whip out their wallets. The news blurbs were also important because they allowed me to talk and talk about politics.

There were times when Ellen wanted me to share the numbers from the day before. We would often recognize the canvassers who had performed well the previous day to a round of applause. And then sometimes I just felt like saying stupid things that would get people to laugh. One time I welcomed everyone to D.C., saying it was the Nation's Capital, the Beltway, the Windy City, the Emerald City, the Big Easy, the Big Apple, the Little Apple, and the Gateway to the West. Little things like these were meaningless, but I enjoyed them. I would often think of little ways to make people laugh while I lay in bed for sleep the night before. I would giggle aloud and wish it was morning already when I knew just the right thing to say. Everyone knew these speeches lacked meaning, but I think they helped people loosen up from their morning commute and put them in the right mindset to start a day of canvassing. And they allowed me to talk.

When announcements were over, I would led the OT's outside. We would go down into the median and start practicing the rap. OT's were not sent out to work unless they had mastered the rap. Each was told during his or her initial interview to memorize the script, but few did. I had them form up a circle and asked each to recite it. I started to give them an example, and I would let the script flow out with all the emphasis I used in the street. I read the OT's as I recited it to see who thought I was performing a superhuman feat of memorization and who was looking at me confidently. Then we would go around the circle to see who was ready to canvass, who might be ready to canvass, and who should not go out.

As the Korean Veteran illustrates, the demographics of these groups were unpredictable. There would be rich, bright college kids standing next to a high school dropout or a newly arrived immigrant or a weary adult bouncing from job to job. Most of them made the same mistakes. They would ask if they could improvise. I would shake my head. It wasn't a good idea for your first day and we were contractually obligated to use the rap provided by our Godfather Howard Dean at the DNC. They would also get nervous. This would be the first clue that an OT should not be sent out to canvass that day. If they were nervous or unsure of the script in front of me, there was no way they could stop strangers in the street and do it. The ones who hadn't learned the rap had to leave immediately. To send them out would be a waste of money for the DNC and a waste of that person's time. I learned later on that allowing someone to canvass when they couldn't learn the rap would only make things more painful for that person since they would go through the ordeal of a day of snubbing and feel far worse about themselves than if we just let them go at 9:30.

Sometimes, OT's would appeal to me to let them go out for the day. I remember an African college student named Abraham whose rap was as slow as molasses but who begged me to let him canvass.

"Forgive me, I am nervous," he said, tears in his eyes. "I promise that when I go out there, I will be good." I couldn't say no, so I sent him out. After thirty minutes in the field, he left and never came back.

The OT's who did look as if they could canvass got about thirty more minutes of practicing the rap. I paired people and walked between the groups, giving tips and listening. At about ten, I gathered everyone and asked them to perform the rap for me one last time. This was the final cut, and I often had to dismiss people here as well. By the end of the training, the OT group was usually down to one or two people. I gave the lucky winners blue DNC T-shirts and a clipboard with contributor forms and had them join grab practice, where the other canvassers taught them how to flag down passersby.

We were a sight each morning, a group of DNC t-shirt-clad young people asking each other if we had a minute for the Democrats. We would respond to each other using the same brush-offs we'd have to hear all day, saying that we were already Democrats or that we didn't have any time or that we already gave online.

At about 10:30, Ellen would call everyone back together, and the field managers would announce who was on their teams and where they were going. Then we all put our left hands into the circle instead of the right and did a cheer. Usually we would say "Biyahhh!" for Howard Dean. And then we would jump on the Metro and fan out all over the city. On the way down into the Dupont Circle station, I would read the words of Whitman that were inscribed in stone above the escalator, where "Thus in silence in dreams' projections," he wrote of his time as a Civil War nurse. He recalls "the experience sweet and sad."

We canvassed everywhere we could reach on the Metro. We went downtown to Metro Center and Chinatown and Farragut Square and McPherson Square and we went uptown to Georgetown and Woodley Park and Cleveland Park and Friendship Heights. We went out to Bethesda and Silver Spring in Maryland and Arlington and Alexandria in Virginia. The point was to get anywhere people with money walked around outside as fast as possible and to accost them for money for four and a half to five hours. That made it pretty simple. The city is a horde of prosperous people walking and using the Metro.

That's not to say all the neighborhoods were the same. The more I saw of D.C. and its suburbs, the more I knew that the

Metro can drop you in different worlds in a matter of minutes. You had to understand the dynamics of a neighborhood to be an effective canvasser. Comprehending the social and economic drivers of each area proved to be one of the richest parts of my experience. It was intoxicating to raise money to elect the first black President on U street and it was exhilarating to fundraise in Virginia. Everywhere I went, I found new reasons to feel as if I were in the center of the election. It was an appropriate sensation for the nation's capital.

When we did reach the canvassing site, or "turf," the field manager, the FM, was in charge. He or she would direct everyone in the crew of one to three other people on the makeup of the neighborhood and the best places to stand. Then the FM would point each person to a spot. Lunch time started whenever the FM wanted, and the crew didn't leave the site until the FM indicated that it was time to go. Although I was their boss by technicality, the FM's were in charge of me when I first went out there. They were more experienced and better at canvassing than me. Far from asserting my authority, I wanted to learn as much as I could from them.

They weren't my only resources, though. Bagels constituted a critical aspect of my canvassing. No matter where we went, I found a bagel place to eat lunch. Bagels became another constant for me. I had worked one summer at Einstein Brother's Bagels, and I knew the value of a well-toasted bagel with cream cheese. Plus, I'm Jewish. The truth is that a bagel with cream cheese is packed with sustaining energy that won't run out all day and won't disturb one's constitution. These qualities are essential for any food eaten while canvassing. I looked at my budget and deemed bagels necessary there as well. I saved over $100 a month by eating bagels every day instead of footlong subs or burgers with fries. And so when lunchtime rolled around, I could be found in the Au Bon Pain or the Panera or the Whole Foods chewing that bagel.

I wouldn't have been able to give you an exact time on that, though. Lunchtime came at different times on different days. The flow of the day dictated lunchtime. If we went out there and got ignored and berated for an hour, I took early lunches to get that bagel in me to turn things around. If we had a good morning, they could be later and more leisurely. No matter when it was, though, lunch gave you time to talk to other canvassers. There's a camaraderie one feels with the other people who stand outside all day and bother people for money in the hot sun and the cold glares, and lunch was venting time. Canvassing provides a never-ending stream of stories of triumphs and defeats and pure nonsense. That's why you looked forward to lunch when you were out there and people were making faces at you or ignoring you, or you looked forward to it when people had affirmed your faith in humanity and treated you like a hero. When you rode this mental roller coaster, you couldn't wait to see what became of the others.

Lunch and the Metro ride were the only time I spent not working. The day was for canvassing. I wanted to talk to as many people as possible and raise as much money as I could every minute I was out there. I believe I was rewarded for my labor, not just in terms of funding the campaign, but in the perspectives I gained talking to fifty people a day. When you approach that many strangers, you hear something new all the time. You also, of course, get used to hearing the same thing. I compiled Washingtonians' responses like an anthropologist.

When 4 o' clock rolled around, it was time to return to the office. We went back to the office to "cash out." This was the procedure in which everyone added up what they had raised and completed their paperwork. With a staff of thirty or forty it could be a logistical nightmare. Every canvasser needed a place to sit and write, and there was simply not enough space. We had three piece-of-shit plastic foldout tables and innumerable folding chairs and we set them up in the back room for the staff. Every canvasser would need to complete his or her contributor forms by printing his or her name and date on the bottom. Once that was done, they would report what they had raised to their FM, who would record everything on a crew sheet. Then the FM collected all the forms, all the cash, and all the checks, and confirmed that everything added up. When they finished, we checked their work and let them go.

I realize this sounds simple, but it could be quite difficult. The tables were packed with crews huddled over their clipboards and squinting at each other's forms. Thousands of dollars of cash sat in piles uncounted and unwadded. Human error caused addition mistakes. People were sweaty and tired and wanted to get out of there and would give one wrong figure and the whole process could be gummed up. The phone would ring off the hook and the downstairs buzzer would sound. The bathroom might get disgusting or clogged.

OT's would be smack in the middle of this chaos, more bewildered than at the start of the day. If they had survived the day, I tried to make them feel at ease. I saw to it that none of them would be sitting around wondering whether they could leave. The end of the day was when I would let them know if we would invite them back to be a member of the staff. If they had raised at least $130, then they were automatically new staff members. Anything less and I had authority not to invite them back. The decision was usually clear. If the person looked as if he or she had been run over by a freight train, they would not want to be invited back and I wouldn't do so. If they looked disappointed and hungry and eager to learn, then I would give them another chance. They would get two more days, two more chances to make staff. As a result of the clear choice, there was rarely an incident when I had to let someone go.

It was typical of the Sisyphusian nature of the office that I would start interviews right after dismissing people. Our office held information sessions and interviews each night at 6 p.m. As soon as the field managers finished, we propped the tables back up against the wall and set up the folding chairs to accommodate the interviewees. We answered job calls constantly and wrote down the names of interested parties, so we knew how many people to expect. Five to ten people usually showed up. People started filing in at 5:30, and as each one arrived, he or she received a clipboard with an application to fill out. We would tell them on the phone to bring something to write with, but most of the time they forgot and we would have to rummage around the office looking for pens. The interviewees would then sit in the folding chairs jotting down their information on the applications. As they arrived, I prepared for my second public speaking exhibition of the day. I would change out of my sweaty blue DNC T-shirt and into a dry wick shirt, taking time to wash my hands and face.

Preparations were necessary because I had a lot to say. It was my responsibility to perform the "group rap.," an informational oral presentation that kicked off every interview. It lasted ten to fifteen minutes, and I thought of it as a sort of performance every time I did it. It was my chance to introduce Progressive Futures and the D.C. office, and I took it seriously. I started with a brief history of PFI, explaining its roles in the 2004 and 2006 elections. Then I described how PFI fit into the overall Democratic strategy for this year's election and how the DNC would be using the resources we raised. I focused on the neighbor-to-neighbor voter mobilization project that would turn voters out like never before, the voter protection program which would ensure that every vote was counted, and the campaign commercials that would counter right-wing chicanery. I then explained the way our office worked, laying out details like the hours and pay. I did my best to spell out the complicated pay policy in as concise a manner as possible. We had what I called a "quota-based system," whereby each canvasser would get 30% commission for all contributions he or she raised over the weekly pay quota. That figure, which changed every week, was 80% of the office average for that particular week. That means, I said, that for everything you raise below the office quota, you'll get minimum wage for your time, while for everything that you raise above the office quota, you'll get it back in 30% commission.

With all that out of the way, I ended the talks by sharing my story. This was a standard part of this lecture that took place every day in every one of PFI's offices, but it did allow me to inject some of my personality. I related that I thought of myself as a student of history and that I felt that this was an election that would be remembered for generations. It wouldn't be only the election of the first black president. It was a chance to win states like Virginia and North Carolina and Indiana, places no Democrat had won since 1964. This was their chance.

On that note, I excused myself and went back into the front room. I would tell the other directors that I had finished delivering the group wrap and we would set up three to four interview stations by scooting folding chairs together. Then we would each take an interviewee and lead them to the chairs, where we would conduct the five-to-ten minute interview. Not once did I read their completed application. I asked the standard questions, and it was again easy to tell who had what it took. The first cut was the crazy people. There was a certain kind of person who, when asked the simple question of what they thought of the introductory presentation, would launch into an incomprehensible treatise on what was wrong with the world. I would ask most of these people just that one question and let them talk for five minutes before letting them know that we would contact them before noon the next day if we had an opening, our stock answer to people we didn't invite back. The second cut was nervous people. These were people who acted as if my gaze were the glare of network television. If someone was timid when he or she were talking to me, he or she would have no chance with the big shot lawyers near Metro Center. The third cut was felons. We had been instructed not to hire any convicted felons, mostly because Progressive Futures had done so in 2004 and incurred the wrath of the news media, which dubbed the operation "Convicts for Kerry." There was a space on the application to list one's criminal record, and this was the only section I did read every time. The only other people who didn't make it were people who rubbed me the wrong way. I hired several older people, but many oldsters were unfit because they could not meet the physical or mental demands of the job. Many asked if they had to climb the stairs every time they came in to the office and many bragged about their previous experience as if their company were a special privilege. Some people disqualified themselves by having been customer service agents for Verizon because that company handled our office telephones and its operators were unhelpful to the point of being litigious. There were many reasons not to hire people, and all of them seemed justified to me.

But most people got invited back for observation days. I found that our trainer had spoken the truth when she said that anyone who could form a coherent sentence could be a canvasser. Most people have the potential, but it is always a question of whether a person can stand the abuse of canvassing, the grind of being ignored all day by surly people but staying at it long enough to raise some money. Every aspect of the interview process was geared toward inviting in observers, and the interview was like an assembly line. People would be given a folding chair, an application, a ten to fifteen-minute spiel, a five to ten-minute interview followed by a start date, a copy of the rap, and a couple of tax forms. We ran about twenty or so people through this process every day, and we never stopped trying to add new staff.

The end of interviews was usually the end of my duties, but I had to stay until all the directors had completed theirs. Other directors needed to complete the numbers and the daily deposit before anyone could leave. The "numbers" were an electronic record of that day's fundraising. It was a tedious Microsoft Excel-laden process. First, you would reproduce electronic versions of all the crew sheets from the day by entering data onto an Excel spreadsheet. With those e-crews completed, it was time to add up all the totals of the day, in dollars, number of people talked to, number of contributions, and every possible statistic. Once you knew these figures, you would enter onto a spreadsheet known as the "monster" which would use the sums to calculate even more statistics. Then, you would e-mail all the e-crews and the monster to Regional Director Adam Jacobs and the national office.

The daily deposit was more laborious. This process necessitated the checking of all the contributor forms and the cash against the amounts they were supposed to add up to. You would use the crew sheets to see how much each crew reported raising in credit card donations, checks, and cash and ensure that the numbers matched what was there. Then you would add up everything and stack all the forms on top of each other with a piece of paper bearing the totals sitting on top. These forms and money had to go to Boston. First, the cash had to be converted to money orders. You would go over to the drugstore on the circle for those, and then hit up the Fed Ex next door to send away the package. It was a simple process, but the logistics of carrying thousands of dollars around and waiting in lines always made the deposit take longer than you thought it would.

We completed all of these tasks before we left the office each day. Most of the time we would be finished by 8 or 8:30, but there were plenty of days where crises would push everything back an hour. And then of course, there were times when you had to stay for the night crew and you wouldn't leave until 10 or 11.

It was a solid twelve to fifteen-hour day Monday through Friday. Saturdays and Sundays were shorter days, but they were never regular days off. When all was said and done, I found myself having worked roughly eighty hours a week.

I tried not to think about all this when the day was through. It was difficult, though. I would sit on the train, exhausted and consumed by my work. I would listen to the other passengers' conversations and think they were talking about Barack Obama, only to listen closer and find they weren't talking about the election at all. When I transferred at Chinatown and made it back to Pentagon City, I trudged the thirty minutes back to Stan and Jenny's house from the Metro stop. Once there, I could practice my nightly routine and let each day end. But tomorrow couldn't come soon enough.

Chapter 9

Relief

My heart is aching
for them Poles and Greeks
on relief way across the sea
because I was on relief
once in 1933

I know what relief can be-
it took me two years to get on WPA.
If the war hadn't come along
I wouldn't be out of the barrel yet.
Now, I'm almost back in the barrel again.

To tell the truth,
if these white folks want to go ahead
and fight another war,
or even two,
the one to stop 'em won't be me.

Would you?

-Langston Hughes

Barack Obama won the black vote. In near-universal proportions, African-Americans voted for the first black presidential candidate. Yet anyone who thinks his appeal to blacks was monochromatic did not canvass on the streets of D.C.

African-Americans were some of our best contributors. The black guys on staff used to say they guilt-tripped black people to support the first black candidate, and I would estimate that around half of my contributors were black. We won donations from attorneys and analysts, construction workers and consultants, students and teachers, and white people and black people, and every color in between.

Interactions that didn't yield money have left the longest lasting impression on me. On July 30, I was canvassing in the Rosslyn neighborhood of Arlington. A muscle-bound black man in a tank top and workout shorts walked up listening to his earphones. Undeterred, I asked him if he had a minute for the Democrats, but he shook his head and walked by me. Five feet past me, though, he turned and took off his earphones. He propped his leg up on a nearby railing and caught his breath. The sun beat down on his sweating forehead.

"Let me tell you something," he said to me. "The only reason white people will vote for this black man is that they don't want to fight this war."

I met another person who challenged what I thought the black community thought of Barack Obama and the Democrats the next day. I was standing outside of that Starbucks on 14th & P, and I was not feeling the love. We had canvassed there often, and the people who worked in that neighborhood had grown tired of us. They scowled at me when I asked them if they had a minute for the Democrats. One guy who worked at a nearby bar wrinkled his face and wiggled his nose to give me the most disgusted facial expression he could muster. A few minutes after he passed, I thought I saw him coming up P Street again. I squinted in his direction but couldn't tell if it was he until he was a few feet away. Recognizing him, I kept my mouth shut.

Just then, I noticed a woman had come out of Starbucks at nearly the same time the guy from the bar went by. I scolded myself for missing a possible stop and went back to canvassing.

A minute or so later, the woman came back toward me.

"Excuse me," said this large woman in workout clothes. "What are you doing out here?"

"Oh, I'm here for Barack Obama and the Democrats," I said, launching into the rap. "We're working hand in hand to—"

She cut me off. "So why didn't you approach me?"

"Well, I--," I stammered, caught off guard.

"That's it," she said. "I'm through with the Democrats." Then she stormed off, leaving me standing in stunned silence. I got upset with myself for not running after her. I wanted to catch up with her and tell her that I didn't talk to her because I wasn't doing my job well enough. I wanted to tell her that I was tired from working fifteen hours the day before. I wanted to tell her I was sorry. Instead, I stood dumbfounded and upset.

The next day, another angry woman voiced her displeasure. I was at the Starbucks in Dupont Circle having a big day when a fashionable middle-aged woman stopped to talk with me. I didn't get more than the first two sentences of the rap out before she began to harangue me about Barack Obama's background.

"Barack Obama is not African-American," she said in a declarative voice. "He's African. His father came over on a plane. His ancestors did not come to America on a ship like mine did. His mother's family is related to Jefferson Davis. Do you know who Jefferson Davis is?"

"Yes m'am, I do." I said calmly. I had already raised a significant amount of money and I decided that I would humor her by listening. The woman shared her personal story, her belief system, the status of blacks in our society. It was enlightening. Eventually, I stopped her and asked why anyone needed to be pinned down by others' definitions of them.

"You just don't get it," she said and walked away. I laughed. This woman had been far less personal than the one from the day before, but I was proud not to be disturbed by a strange perspective. The more experience I got with the wide range of views, the more I could stay on an even keel.

My negative interactions with blacks while canvassing were the exception, not the rule. D.C.'s significant black population combined with the Obama phenomenon to produce thousands of dollars for the DNC. Within those thousands of dollars, there was a tinge of excitement that America just might elect a black president. I remember one of the other directors, a blonde Virginian named Mary, telling a story about a contribution she got over by Union Station. She said a young black man walked up holding his young child's hand and listened politely to her rap. The man reached into his pocket for a five-dollar bill and he waved it to his son.

"Son, I want you to remember this day," he said. "This is the day I gave money to help elect the first black president." It was a beautiful story, and all the more beautiful because Mary told it in her Southern accent and you knew it happened in the shadow of the Capitol. Moments like these made the election of 2008 what it was. The stakes were such that the days were a constant stream of symbols of what a win could mean for this country. I felt I was on the threshold of history, and I yearned for affirmation in my day-to-day labors.

Validation didn't come often, though, and certainly not from my paycheck. I received about $1,800 per month before taxes. If you allow that I worked an average of 75 hours per week, I was paid about five or six dollars an hour. There's no doubt that I did not enlist to line my wallet, but it was not a living wage. I got by because Stan and Jenny put me up in their house, but without them, I would not have been able to afford rent.

When I got the first full-time paycheck of my adult life on August 1, I wrote out my first budget. I allotted all the funds I would be spending for the upcoming month. My anticipated expenses equaled $600. This depended upon my eating bagels for lunch every day. Since I made about $1,400 per month after taxes, I had about $800 in discretionary income. With no time to spend that money, though, I planned to save $500 per month. I kept meticulous records in pursuit of this goal, noting every dollar I spent each day to keep a running total of how much money I had already spent and how much more I could spend.

The room where I was staying in Stan and Jenny's house had an old rattan table with a mirror on top, and that's where I put the notebook where I recorded my purchases. I would write them down each night and peer into the mirror, amused by the sight. It made me think of where I had been just months before, a well-fed, comfortable college student with no obligations except making grades and getting drunk. Now I ate for sustenance and worked day and night to support myself. I liked looking in that mirror.

Those moments gave me the self-reliance I needed to deal with what was becoming a pressure-filled workplace. Ellen escalated things by calling for us directors to raise $10,000 for the upcoming week. The office-wide goal was $52,000, which was $14,000 more than we had ever grossed. She informed me of these new goals on a Saturday morning before I canvassed, and she told me that she would tell the rest of the directors in a meeting Sunday afternoon. Sunday's meeting didn't go as planned, though. The other five directors and I showed up at 4:30, the scheduled time. We were annoyed by the necessity of commuting on a Sunday afternoon, and Ellen galled us all the more by not showing up. She just left a sheet of paper with the goals on it and requested us to discuss how we would meet them.

We did have a discussion, but it did not regard how we could achieve these numbers. Instead, we talked about how outlandish these figures were and about how unrealistic it was to hold ourselves to these standards. We left resolved to tell Ellen on Monday that these goals would not be reachable. Of course, that plan didn't come to fruition either. Monday is the worst day of the week for canvassing, both in numbers and attitude. People are more likely to be in a bad mood or unable to take their minds off work long enough to make donations. Predictably, then, we had a rough day that Monday. Those goals seemed even more out of touch with reality than before.

Ellen gathered us to talk after we had finished interviews that night, and she was unfazed. She was disappointed with us. We began the meeting by sharing how much money each of us had raised that day, and nobody had raised more than $100.

"Guys, this is terrible," Ellen said. "If we keep doing this badly, I'm going to have to start firing people." I looked around at the other directors' faces, and there were looks of shock and dismay. Nobody said anything about the impossibility of the goals, and Ellen reiterated them once more.

"We're going to canvass day and night until we reach these goals, guys," she said. It was at that moment that I knew that her eyes were different in nature than I had originally believed. They were a deep brown, and she could use them to communicate such empathy and sweetness. When she looked at you the right way, she could make you want to cry tears of joy. Now, though, I saw that those eyes had other applications. They could be used for firmness and insistence. She looked at us this way and we were compelled to agree. It didn't matter that the goals made no sense, that PFI directors are almost never fired, and that, by this time the following week, we no longer spoke of these numbers. At that moment, we had to raise that money.

The threat was not real, though. It was obvious that directors would not be fired at the drop of a hat or even at the drop of their canvassing totals. It's such a low-paying, grueling job that few are willing to do it. Those willing to take it on usually can stay for as long as they want. During my meditative routine that night, I realized that it was not in my interest to antagonize Ellen. She had little say in PFI's prerogatives, but she had more of a say than I did. If I rebelled against her control, I would lose an ally in my relationship with national headquarters. Then I'd be sent anywhere with nobody to intervene on my behalf. Plus, I felt that, deep down, Ellen was just a sweet motherly person who had to take out her stress on others at times.

I thought this because of the times she wanted to confide in me. I never would have shared personal details about myself with her, but every now and again, she shared hers with me in a way that I found endearing. Her fiancé, a French guy named Jean-Pierre who looked to be in his mid-thirties, was visiting her. They hadn't seen each other for months, so Jean-Pierre maximized his time with her by lounging about the office. He never bothered anyone, he mostly just sat in front of one of the computers and checked out his stocks on the Internet. And he was nice enough to move if anybody needed to use the computer for something office-related. All the women in the office told Ellen he was cute and I told her he seemed like a cool guy, because I knew that's what she wanted me to say. One day, Ellen took me aside.

"Hey Toby," she said. "I need to talk to you about something. Do you know how long it's been since Jean-Pierre and I have seen each other?"

Not sure why she would ask me this, I answered, "Several months, right?"

"Yea," she said. "Almost a year. And it sucks that I have to be here all the time to look over everybody's shoulders. What I would really like would be to be able to get away for an hour or two at a time with him." I said I could understand why she didn't want to sit in her office all day instead of seeing D.C. with her fiancé.

"Exactly," she said. "You're the best, thanks for understanding. Do you think you can keep things in check around here while I'm out? You're picking everything up so quickly, and everybody really respects the way you approach each day."

"Thanks, Ellen," I said. "I'd be glad to." And I was touched, not by Ellen's compliments, which were attached to her asking for leeway to hang out with her fiancé, but by the fact that she was not afraid of being seen together with him. She was not afraid to devote herself to another person. It didn't make any difference to me if she wanted to break away from the office for a couple hours a day while he was in town, and her dedication to Jean-Pierre had no bearing on the fact that she was a strong, independent woman running a campaign office. She didn't care if I or other people said or thought that she was just another foolish American girl mistaking a foreign accent for profundity. I respected her for letting love flow over her in a way that others wouldn't because of potential temporary discomforts.

That's why I was glad to be there a few days later when she became anxious about the wedding. She called me aside again, and her big eyes were overflowing with tears.

"Toby," she said as tears rolled down her face. "I don't know about this. I just don't know about this. How am I supposed to know if I'm going to love Jean-Pierre for the rest of my life?" I couldn't imagine why I was the one she had decided to reveal this to, but I didn't show it. I just tried to calm her down.

"You can't know, Ellen, nobody knows," I said. "How could anyone possibly explain why they love another person or predict what person they will love at what time? Nobody gets to choose. It's out of our control."

"That's what makes this so scary," she said.

"I know, but we have to try because it's all we've got. Listen, has something happened during Jean-Pierre's visit?"

"No, it's been great."

"Well, then all you can do is know that he's willing to make the commitment to try to love you the rest of his life and be willing to make the same commitment." She thanked me and dried her tears. We went back into the other rooms with everyone else. The words I said to pacify her came from no experience whatsoever in these matters, and they represented what I thought to be true instead of what I knew to be true. But I'm glad that they worked to cool her anxiety before she did something regretful. I've always felt it my duty to move people together, to say things that will result in greater unification and not less. In this instance, my efforts were successful.

But episodes like these were why I never felt enmity towards Ellen, and never tried to challenge her when she laid down the law. She was subject to personal difficulties and pressure from above her at Progressive Futures just like me. I learned later why there was always an emphasis on directors raising money when I learned the terms of PFI's contract with the DNC. As I understand it, PFI received a certain amount of money for each canvasser who completed a daily shift. PFI used part of this amount to pay the commissions that canvassers received. What made the contract financially viable for both parties was the labor of directors like me. Directors raised more money on average than canvassers, and we didn't receive commission. Therefore, when I badgered 350 bucks out of passersby in the fashionable Dupont area, I was lining the pockets of both Howard Dean and PFI. It's no wonder, then, that directors were pressured to bring home the bacon. We all demanded a lot of ourselves and we did want to lead the office by example, but the pressure from above us in the PFI hierarchy was the product of that contract.

That knowledge would have helped me on that Monday when I was canvassing in the Dupont area. I raised a paltry $20 from a weekday crowd of people who were tired of seeing us. But I did get to meet E.J. Dionne. The *Post* columnist passed by me using a stock excuse that he is a journalist, a foolish reaction not just because it is not a yes or no response to the question of whether you have a minute for the Democrats, but also because it implies that the golden calf of objectivity in journalism could be obtained if journalists did not speak to canvassers. I recognized him, though, so I got him to stop and chat. I had seen him on *The News Hour with Jim Lehrer* and read his columns for many years, so it was a thrill. I asked him what he thought of Obama's chances, but he was non-committal. He spoke of Obama's actions and decisions as if it is the job of a presidential candidate to prove himself righteous to the pundits.

Dionne is one of my favorite columnists, but I hated him at that moment. He wrote columns praising the Democrats and advocating for Obama, and he rallied support among liberals. Yet, he had no stake in the election. If Obama had lost, his life would be the same. He would still ruminate upon the day's news. He might regret the loss or rue it, but it wouldn't have been his failure. He didn't stand in the heat all day and spoil peoples' walks by confronting them with the reality of the election again and again. He didn't make a personal investment in the election that the man with the child who gave $5 did. And he didn't look at every day as an opportunity to ensure victory for the Democrats in November. All he did was write columns. There is value to that, but there wasn't when I was getting snubbed all day in Dupont, and all he could do was speak in vagaries to someone he should have inspired.

Chapter 10

From A Consecration

Others may sing of the wine and the wealth and the mirth,
The portly presence of potentates goodly in girth;-
Mine be the dirt and the dross, the dust and scum of the earth!

Theirs be the music, the color, the glory, the gold;
Mine be a handful of ashes, a mouthful of mold.
Of the maimed, of the half and the blind in the rain and the cold-
Of these shall my songs be fashioned, my tales be told.

-John Masefield

Mary Jane Martin called me two names: "boo" and "baby." She called everyone by those two names. Whenever someone addressed her, she'd answer back, "What, baby?" or "Yes, boo?" It was an odd but endearing habit, and Mary Jane is one of my favorite people.

The pedestrians of Georgetown did not feel the same way about her. We were on M Street on a steamy August day, and nobody had the time of day for a biracial hippie who didn't shave her pits. Nobody had the time of day for me, either. We didn't give a damn. We blocked peoples' paths between a Starbucks and a French restaurant on the narrow brick sidewalks that get packed with pedestrians. It was summer, but the glares could not have been icier. We brought back a pittance for the party that day.

Mary Jane was a director, just like me. Whenever I felt like complaining about PFI's treatment of me, I thought of her before I said anything. She lived in the office for two to three weeks, sleeping on an old couch in the back. It was a violation of human rights. She didn't have any place to stay in D.C., and Progressive Futures didn't put people up anywhere.

I don't know how she endured, but it didn't seem to bother her. She never once complained. She only whipped her curly black hair around and made everyone around her smile. Mary Jane was jovial and sweet, and if those Georgetown snobs have a problem with Mary Jane, they can go to hell. They lost the election and we won.

I depended on Mary Jane more and more because we lost four directors in one fell swoop. The voter registration campaign materialized, and our office became smaller. The Boston office called in hundreds of directors nationwide to train for "voter reg," as we called it, and I've never seen any of these people again. That's not to imply that they died, but the rapidity of it was mind-boggling. The exodus exemplified the irony of Progressive Futures. We were told again and again to get people to buy into our vision and to believe in us as people. Yet, any time the national office decided that the priorities had changed, we were to forget our people and move on to develop a new group. Canvassers came up to me with bewildered expressions, wondering why their directors had left without a word yesterday and where they would be. I had no good answers.

I did have a good answer, however, when Adam asked me to be part of the voter reg campaign. It was no. I had made up my mind that I was staying in D.C., so I told him how much I liked the people in this office and working in this city and that I had found my home here. He laughed. He laughed at everything I said to the point that it was obvious that he wasn't listening. When he did understand that I was not interested in voter reg, he ended the conversation as soon as he could. He had plenty more people to call, so I didn't matter. There were people willing to hang up and start packing, and he needed to get to them.

With fewer people around, my role simplified. It was at this time that I began to focus on staff development. The interviews were always interesting, that's for sure. One time, a large, scantily clad black woman named Babs showed up to canvass for us. She said she had been hired, but couldn't name the director who interviewed her or what day she interviewed. It was obvious that she never interviewed, so we invited her to come and interview at 6 p.m. that night. I hadn't met her before she came in, so I was somewhat surprised when she sashayed in at 5:15 wearing stilettos and carrying three parasols. She sat in a folding chair and said she would love some water. Nobody said anything back, so she sat for a long time. It was not out of the ordinary for an interviewee to show up abnormally early like this, so nobody paid her any mind, even though she had her sunglasses on indoors and sat with her legs apart to share an unseemly view with the world.

Finally, it was time to interview her. She confided to me that she was glad to come up here because "all the guys in the restaurant downstairs wouldn't stop staring at me." I gave her a blank expression, but she just kept talking. Babs related the story of her last job, as manager in an office where she fired half the staff on her first day. She said her boss backed up her decisions and gave her a promotion. She explained that she actually wanted McCain to win, but she liked Obama and wanted to see what he had to offer. She told me that she would take over this office. She spoke for about twenty minutes in this vein, and I had asked her only what she thought of my presentation. This woman would have scared the bejesus out of everyone she talked to, so it was an easy decision. I told her I would call her by noon tomorrow if we had an opening for her. She told me that she expected my call.

I thought this was the last time I would see Babs, but she kept turning up. Her boyfriend worked for us for a while. He was a skinny white guy, and he wore one of those leather dog collars around his neck. There was something strange about that relationship. When payday came around, Babs would appear to demand his Metro reimbursement check, which never seemed to be there. While other directors rummaged through the huge stack of checks so that this terrifying woman would be satisfied, she would look at me and say "I'm still waiting on that call, Toby. I never got that call. What happened?" I would shrug and deal with something else, but she asked me every time she was in. One time, the guy had not brought any money for the Metro, so I offered to loan him three bucks. He got a worried look and stammered that his girlfriend didn't like him borrowing money. He decided to call Babs and proceeded to plead with her to allow him to borrow three dollars. I guess he convinced her because he took my money, but that was the last day he worked for us. The next payday, he and Babs showed up at the office to pick up his last paycheck. She handed me three dollars to repay me and apologized for his laziness. That was the last time I saw Babs, but I have a feeling she's going to turn up again one of these days.

Not everyone was crazy, of course. Some great people interviewed with us, and they could do more than form coherent sentences. There was a woman who had a master's degree in political science and wanted to get involved while she pursued her Ph.D. We had a great conversation. A couple days later, a thank-you note appeared in the mail, and I still have it. She wrote, "Your energy and excitement about the Democratic Party is extremely affirming and I look forward to working with you." Then there was a former television journalist and campaign manager who handed out his blog address to everyone during the information session. He told me about his days chasing Scott Peterson around and said that I had a future in front of a camera.

Another one of my favorites was a black high school kid named Jeffrey. He was the last interviewee one night, and he wanted to ask me some questions. He took out a stack of note cards, on which he had taken notes from a Christopher Hitchens book. He asked me if I believed in God and, if so, how I could go about proving it. I said that I did, but that I couldn't prove it, that the coincidental nature of life can only be explained by a force beyond the scope of reason or logic. He agreed and we went back and forth for several minutes. I just shrugged when the other directors asked me what had taken so long on the last interview. I hired all these people, but not one of them worked a day for us.

Such was the nature of PFI interviews. I took steps to combat it. I used to keep all the applications of the good people to call or email them the night of the interview to tell them how excited I was to have them come on board. It rarely made a difference. The quality people understood that everyone who could form coherent sentences would be hired, and they envisioned far better opportunities for themselves than badgering people for money on the street. I can't blame them.

But I was always amazed by the number of people looking for jobs in our office. Twenty and thirty people packed themselves into the little room in the back where I held our information sessions. Some people brought their whole family, and little kids would run around the office, not sure of where they were. It was depressing to see how many people can be lured by the possibility of a low-paying, dead-end job.

Not everyone wanted to work for me, though. Eddie Kliensasser definitely wasn't interested. He invited me out one Saturday night to the Georgetown waterfront, one of his new favorite places to get drunk. I couldn't break away from the office until early in the evening, so I found him sitting under an umbrella at a Mexican restaurant's outdoor patio. He was wearing a Burberry polo shirt and boat shoes, and I could tell from the redness of his face that he had been drinking a long time.

"Tobes!" he said when he spotted me. "What the hell took you so long? Sit down, order up a beer, you've got some catching up to do."

"That's obvious," I said, sitting down at the table. "I got here as quick as I could, but some people need to work for a living."

"That sucks, man. I've been drinking all day with my roommates out here. They went up the street to somebody's party, but I told them I had to stay and meet an old friend of mine."

"Wow. Eddie, that was sweet of you. I sure appreciate it." I said it in a patronizing voice, but I meant it, too. Eddie wasn't in the mood for subtleties, though.

"Why don't you shut the fuck up and check out those blondes over there?" He motioned to a group of buxom debutantes in sundresses on the other side of the dock. Gorgeous women were a dime a dozen down there, dressed to sit out in the sun and sip multi-colored cocktails. It was a nice setup, if not tasteful. The paved sidewalk led to a wooden walkway where ferries and power boats docked, and a massive tiered fountain stood in the middle of four or five restaurants that curved around to close off the area from the rest of the city. Off in the distance, I could see the Kennedy Center and the Watergate looming above the Potomac. Eddie and I sipped Negra Modelos and ate chips and salsa. My parents would have had a field day with the salsa because, instead of being salsa, it was merely mango with bits of cilantro sprinkled on top. Eddie took breaks from shoveling out the mango to make sure I noticed every woman who walked past our table.

"So how's the job search, Eddie?" I asked him.

"Jobs? Why are you bringing up jobs, man? Nobody wants to talk about jobs on a Saturday night." I laughed.

"Well, I assume you've been looking for one."

"Not really. My aunt will find me one someday and my parents seem fine with paying my bills for the time being. So I'm just going to go with it. Jesus, did you see the tits on that blonde who just walked by?"

"I did. She's not my type, though." I was trying to get a rise out of him. It worked. Eddie's eyes bulged out of his sunburned face.

"Not your type? How can you say that? How could she not be your type?"

"Blondes have never seemed interested in me, Eddie. I think it's because I'm not most attracted to them."

"That may be true, but you have to admit that one was hot."

"Alright," I relented. "She was hot."

"Not your type, gimme a break. You wouldn't like the people I hang around with very much. Most of them are Republicans, and all of them hate Obama. One of the guys who lives in my house actually works for the McCain campaign. It gets annoying, so I have to remind them sometimes that at least one person in the house is going to vote for Obama."

"Thanks for sticking up for the cause, Eddie." He caught my sarcasm

"But I don't always. We've been going out to this bar called Smith Point. It's ultra-expensive and exclusive. You've got to be on the list for the night to get in." One of my friends from Progressive Futures who went to Georgetown had told me about that bar as an example of everything he hated about Georgetown, and I could tell that I would have detested it as well. The ironic thing about "the list" was that my friend also told me that anyone could get on the list by calling the bar ahead of time or going to its website. I didn't tell Eddie, though. When Eddie Kliensasser was drinking, there was no interrupting him, and his testosterone-driven thirst for a good time was a throwback to college.

"Whenever we go out there, I tell girls I work for the German embassy or for a Republican congressman. The other day, I told a girl that I'm John Boehner's deputy press secretary, and we ended up making out in the middle of the bar. And she gave me a perfect blow job later." I couldn't hold back any longer.

"But, Eddie, now you can't see her ever again because you lied about what you do for a living, which is actually nothing."

"So what, man? At least I got my dick sucked." I laughed at his vehemence and vulgarity, but I couldn't have disagreed with him more.

"What's the point? She won't do it again once she finds out you lied to her. If you hadn't lied, you might be able to see her again and start something meaningful instead of just being a frat boy your whole life."

"And who wants to do that? Nobody's looking for a relationship here, man. These girls are looking for a good time just as much as I am. You gotta lie to them or they won't think you're shit."

"Really? That's how you get them?"

"Well, only partly. You gotta exaggerate to get them in the sack. 'Something meaningful?' I'm sorry, man, but your perception of love makes me want to fucking puke." The way he snarled as he delivered the last line almost put beer through my nose.

"Well, Eddie, your perception of love makes me want to puke, too. But, as you will be quick to point out, women are a lot more disposed to it than mine." He smiled, and we clanked the beers together and drank more.

Eddie was missing out, though. He didn't get to experience the day I had on August 7th in Adams Morgan. It was the first time I'd been back since my training. It's a vibrant place. You can tell by the Ethiopian restaurants and the live music and the teenybopper bars and African crafts stores, but you can also tell by the people. They were generous that day, shelling out $219 to me for the Democrats. It was the first time I raised over $200 on a weekday.

The day began on the walk from Dupont down to Adams Morgan on Columbia Road. A middle-aged man sitting on a bench flagged me down to ask what I was doing. He filled out the form and handed me a $20 bill.

"I was like you at one time," he said. "I was a yippie with Abbie Hoffman back in the Sixties. Cherish this time because you're going to remember this election the rest of your life."

It was a great way to start the day. I stood outside a Starbucks on the corner of 18th and Columbia, and the flow of people was remarkable. My first contributor was a homeless man. He was mentally imbalanced in some way and his hair was shaved in an odd horseshoe-like shape on the top of his head. I tried to decline his dollar, but he insisted on helping Barack Obama. His contribution form was barely legible, but he was proud to get his pink receipt with an Obama picture on it. I also spoke my broken Spanish just well enough to get $5 from a man who spoke no English and won enough rapport to get $2 from an out-of-work carpenter. There is no comparison between these contributions and the $20 bill that a lawyer hands me like it's his dirty laundry.

I will argue again and again that these people have made a personal investment with this party. I'm not saying that $5 makes the difference in elections, or even that $20, $50, or $100 does, but when someone gets involved financially, they feel they have taken some ownership of the party. They will identify with the fate of Barack Obama and the Democrats. They will pay closer attention after they have paid their membership dues. When I added up the money I raised in the course of the election, the total came to over $17,000. It's great to see a number like that and know that a campaign field office costs roughly $5,000 to run and that conceivably there were three more field offices as a direct result of my work. But it's infinitely more satisfying to think that I politicized a smidge of the proletariat.

That's why I didn't lose my cool when an old guy accused me of forcing people to pay for their votes.

"That's what's wrong with politics today," he said. "It's all about money. You don't just expect people to vote for you anymore, you expect them to pay for millions of dollars of campaigning when they can't afford it because you weren't there for them in the first place." Before I could tell him that I wasn't forcing anyone to do anything and that I was trying to educate people, he crossed the street to make the light.

He didn't get under my skin because I knew he was wrong. The most memorable interactions of the day didn't net me anything. There was a scruffy guy sitting in a Starbucks chair who had on a torn yellow T-shirt that read, "Never forget Katrina." He watched me canvass for a few minutes, then he called me over.

"Say, man, what are you doing out here?"

I told him.

"Well, I'm not in a position to make any donations, but I wanted to talk to you. You remind me of myself circa 1962. I was down in South Carolina trying to register people to vote. We look different, but I can see myself in you." I thanked him and we talked for a little while. If I could go back to that moment, I would have asked him so many more questions.

I think I got it right with the next group that sat under the Starbucks umbrella. A pair of street sweepers took a break to get out of the sun, and they watched me trying to stop people. One of them motioned to me.

"Are you here for Barack Obama?"

I said I was, and I told him what I was doing.

"That's interesting, man. Listen, I want Barack Obama to win, but I'm not going to vote for him."

"Why's that?"

"I'm a felon, I'm not allowed to vote. I've been in jail and I'm through breaking the law. I'm just trying to do whatever I can to live." He said this in the calm voice of a person who has come to terms with the vicissitudes of life. He was a street sweeper, content to smoke away a black and mild and an afternoon in the company of a friend, and I wanted to hear what he had to say.

"I know I'm supposed to root for Barack Obama because he's the first black candidate and all that, and I am, but deep down I know he's just another politician. You know, another party can take over and write new laws and put new people in power, but, for me, life will be the same. I'm going to be a street sweeper no matter if there's a black president or not."

I said I understood where he was coming from, that Barack Obama was a politician running for office like any before him. But I told him that I couldn't agree about this election not changing things. I said we could get universal health insurance. We could make college affordable enough for everyone to attend. We could end the war. Our personal circumstances might stay the same, but we could change this country.

The two guys told me they appreciated what I was doing, and they even said they wanted to donate money on some other day. I doubt if they did, but I wonder what they think of what I said. I wonder if they think about what I said. I know I remember what that guy said to me, and I know I remember what I told him. And I know that this election will be a waste if I wasn't right.

These two conversations kept me going all day, along with a Starbucks ice coffee that some repeat donors bought for me. I learned that day that when I have caffeine in my system I can speak as loud and as long and as fast as I want to. I rarely canvassed without drinking coffee again. It was one of those humid August days, but I never thought of stopping.

Near the end of the day, a woman stopped in the middle of a crowd and looked at me with a quizzical expression.

"Yes, what are you doing?" she asked in a foreign accent.

I told her, and she frowned.

"I'm from Ethiopia and I'm not a citizen yet. I want to vote for Obama, but I can't." She started for the door, but I didn't miss a beat. I let her know how she could get her voice in this election. She said she'd think about it and went into the store. I thought I had lost her, but she came back out of the store five minutes later. She was holding a check in her hand.

"I decided to do it," she said. The check was for $100.

It was one of those days in canvassing when you dream that all the world's a friend. Canvassing is the worst and best job in the world, depending on the day. There are days when people shake their heads at you before you can even say hi, and then there are days when canvassing can be the perfect intersection of labor and its reward. On the latter type of days, the sun pounds down until you find your face caked in the salt of your sweat and you know that your perspiration has come from a worthy cause. On that Friday in Adams Morgan, I felt ecstatic in exertion.

Chapter 11

From Washington Monument by Night

The wind bit hard at Valley Forge one Christmas.
Soldiers tied rags on their feet.
Red footprints wrote on the snow…
… and stone shoots into stars here
… into half-moon mist tonight.

Tongues wrangled dark at a man.
He buttoned his overcoat and stood alone.
In a snowstorm, red hollyberries, thoughts,
he stood alone.

-Carl Sandburg

I made an old woman cry. I'd been on this Earth forty or fifty years fewer than Velma, but what I said to her on a Friday afternoon in Bethesda made tears stream down her face.

She was yet another Observer. I shouldn't have sent her out to canvass because her rap was not convincing and she didn't seem ready for the physical demands of canvassing. But the thought of a grandma helping to elect Barack Obama proved too romantic for me to turn down. Plus, when I asked everyone to name his or her favorite Motown artist during question of the day, she chose Marvin Gaye, just like me.

The people of Bethesda are not this sentimental, though. Canvassers hound shoppers in the Bethesda Row outdoor mall every day of the week, so people there have no particular problem with shooing canvassers away like gnats. The upside is that the people who don't feel like doing that will donate thousands and thousands of dollars. Canvassers need to be strong-willed and well-acquainted with snubbing to succeed here, so it's not an ideal place for people with little or no canvassing experience.

Progressive Futures was a lot for Velma to handle. She knew she needed to raise $130 to make staff, and she was worried about it. She peppered me with questions on the way over about how many chances she would get and whether she would be invited back if she didn't get $130. I did my best to calm her down and set her up next to an Ann Taylor in a pedestrian walkway. I canvassed up the block from her for about thirty minutes or so before coming back to check on her.

She seemed discouraged. She had only a dollar, and very few people were paying her any mind.

"Can I just quit for today and come back on Monday?" she asked me. I said no, that if she left the site she would not be asked back. She looked disappointed, but she decided to stick it out. I encouraged her for a few minutes before I went back up the block to my position.

When I came back an hour or so later, she was ecstatic. She had gotten a $50 donation, and she had such a big smile. I congratulated her, but I had to remind her that she was still a ways away from $130. I did so in as delicate a manner as possible by telling her that if she got one more contribution, we would have her back on Monday. Her smile disappeared.

"What was that?" she asked.

I repeated myself.

"Does that mean I won't be allowed to come back if I don't get any more donations?" Tears began to roll down her cheeks. I didn't know what to say, so I just apologized. The training book PFI gave me never mentions how to deal with a person who got involved with a simple desire to help elect Barack Obama when he or she realizes that the bottom line is what must define a fundraising office. I just stayed with Velma until she regained her composure and indicated that she wanted to keep going.

She got one more donation, a $5 bill, so she did come back on Monday. She fell far short of the goal then, too, and I knew I had prolonged this whole episode and intensified the painfulness of it for her by letting her canvass. If I had simply sent her home on her first day instead of letting her go out to Bethesda with me, she would have the simple frustration of being rejected. Since she worked those two days, though, she had the humiliating experience of a twenty-something white boy threatening her with being fired as well as not measuring up to my rigid demands. Velma was another reason why I needed to be confident in the people who canvassed for us. I can't say I handled her the right way, but I can at least say I learned from her.

I learned from Vivica too. Vivica was an attractive middle-aged black woman who had bounced around as a singer and actress. She wore head wraps of various colors and called people "sister" and brother." Everyone liked her because she told us stories of protests and campaigns past. She was the kind of person with intelligence borne of a variety of experiences. Vivica often got disgruntled by the hypocritical manner of people who donated far less than they should. It's a common frustration in canvassing, and I did my best to keep her spirits high by talking with her about the importance of our work.

One time, my support for her demanded action instead of words. It was a sunny Saturday, and we were canvassing in Dupont again. I set up at the Starbucks just off the circle, and Vivica was by the Starbucks a couple blocks down Connecticut Avenue. I was doing well, so I walked down to check on her, but Vivica was nowhere to be found. I checked a new voicemail message on my phone. It was Vivica, and she was in hysterics to the point that I could barely make out her words. I did understand that she was back in the office, so I ran back up there to find out the problem. I found her on the stairs above Zorba's with her head buried in her hands. She told me what had happened. She had been canvassing when a man in a BMW honked his horn and called her over to his car. Since canvassing entails a willingness to accommodate anyone who is willing to make a donation, she didn't think twice about approaching the car. She was horrified to find that the man was naked from his waist down and masturbating. Vivica quickly moved away from the vehicle and changed locations, but the man followed her around the neighborhood. She finally just came back to the office to get away from him. I called 911 right away and they asked for a description of the car, which I was able to get from Vivica, but they said a license plate number would be the best way to track down the car. Luckily, the guy was still parked on Connecticut, so I was able to give the number to the police right away. I went back upstairs and told Vivica the good news.

She wrapped her arms around me and said, "Toby, you are a gem." I'll never forget that.

I would have understood if Vivica never came back to canvass again, but she did. She kept at it for a couple more weeks before calling it quits. I remember the morning she called me to tell me that she wouldn't be coming in anymore. I tried everything to convince her to come back, but it was just before 9 a.m. and Ellen started motioning for me to wrap it up even though she knew who I was talking to. I hated Ellen at that moment, but I know why she didn't care whether this remarkable woman would ever come back again.

PFI didn't need her. There would be another thirty people coming to the office to interview that day, so we could send one of those people out in Vivica's place. Her disappointment with people kept her from being a great canvasser, so she wasn't raising that much money. It would be more productive for the office to send someone new out and train that person to be a better canvasser.

I knew this, but it hurt me to see so many people like Vivica cycle in and out of my life in three and four-week intervals. These were bright and motivated people. They would be excited to do this work, but the physical and mental demands would wear them down. A month or so later, they couldn't take it any more and would move on, and the cycle would repeat itself. Our office chewed up and spit out people who could have played large roles.

I understood the situation better once I understood the terms of the DNC's contract with Progressive Futures. The lump sum that the DNC gave to PFI for each canvasser sent out each day meant that the emphasis was on quantity, not quality. We would generate thirty or forty new hires every week in a state of perpetual hiring. But we would only retain five or six of those people beyond their first week, and even fewer after that. It's not possible to give someone the support he or she needs to master canvassing when the phone keeps ringing and it keeps becoming time for the next round of interviews. The contradictions here are obvious, and so is PFI's intention to make a profit.

Yet the sessions also introduced me to Albertine O'Connell. One night when I was delivering another information session, I noticed a gorgeous freckled girl with brown hair tied in a complicated pony-tail smiling at me as I spoke. I grinned back in the way that I did for anyone who showed enthusiasm during my speech and in the way I especially do when a woman has acknowledged me. She looked Irish and intelligent and fun. Weeks later, as we lay in bed, she told me how she remembered that I was wearing an Adidas dry-wick shirt, and she thought to herself, "He's cute." It was stunning to me then, just as it is now, how you can have no notion that someone has noticed you, no suspicion that she will be in your arms someday. And it warms my heart to know that Albertine noticed me that day while I was unaware.

She interviewed with Mary Jane, who gave me her name. I wrote it down along with the phone number from her application. I called her, just as I did anyone who interviewed and seemed eager and bright and looked like he or she had a chance to be good canvassers. I left a message on her voicemail telling her that we were looking forward to her coming into the office for her first day, just like everyone else. And I thought nothing of it.

I didn't spend my days ruminating. I was canvassing, and I had improved by my fourth week in the office. I developed a stock response for all the people who told me that they already gave directly to Obama's campaign. It was a common answer, and you could always tell people thought that their donation to Obama, real or imaginary, meant that I would bid them adieu to let them enjoy their day instead of badgering them for money. They were wrong. A previous donation to Obama was actually the best indicator that this person was willing to give to the DNC, and I didn't know this until I came up with my response.

"That's great," I would say in my most enthusiastic voice. "That's the kind of support it's going to take for Obama to win the White House." Here the person would look at me with a polite and satisfied face, imagining our conversation was coming to a close soon. "However, the best way to complement and supplement your generous support for the Obama campaign is by giving to the DNC, and here's why. The DNC is the party's ground game, conducting operations that will deliver the most voters of all time to the polls on November 4th and ensure that their votes will be counted. These two operations were our biggest problems in 2004, and we can only reverse the results of that year if we have the resources. And that's why I say that the DNC complements and supplements the Obama campaign, and that's why I'll ask you to give to the DNC." The person would either say yes or no, and they said yes many times. Tried and true scripted responses to expected excuses are integral to successful canvassing.

So is building rapport. I could speak about politics in a way that would assure people that I was not a moron just because my office was the sidewalk and my only tool was a clipboard. That's half the battle. The other half is a personal connection. If there was any way that I could find something in common with someone, I did. On the advice of one of our best canvassers, I sometimes incorporated the fact that I was a student from Austin, Texas, into my rap. People like the idea of supporting a student who is working for a good cause, and it was very successful with anyone who had spent time in the Lone Star state. One of the first people I mentioned my alma mater to was a woman who had attended Texas A&M. We chatted about the rivalry and agreed that this election was more important than the football games that were supposed to make us hate each other. She wrote a $200 check. There was a guy that same day who was not interested in talking about Texas but was sporting a T-shirt with a picture of The Band's eponymous album. Before I rapped him, we chatted about all the great songs on that record, and he was happy to contribute twenty bucks to put a black man in the White House.

Both these connections are superficial. I'll never see these people again, and I used the empathy we felt for one another to make them get out their wallets. But that doesn't change the fact that it is possible to make a connection with a stranger in far less time than you can imagine and it doesn't change the fact that conversations like the ones I was having were what won the election. In the swing states and the big cities, there were countless young people like me convincing their elders by going door to door, arguing again and again for a new direction, and working harder than they had ever worked for anything. Obama and the Dems would have won without me, but they wouldn't have won without people like me.

All the days were not this fulfilling. Many were infuriating, like a Sunday that I thought I would be free to host my brother, who was in town for a wedding. I explained to Ellen why I wanted off that Sunday without making the obvious but moot argument that God and the U.S. government allowed a day of rest for all people. She agreed to let me have the day off, but she insisted that I come to the office for a directors meeting at 5 p.m.

My brother came bearing permission from my parents to take me out to eat with our parents' credit card, and I wasn't going to let a meeting put a damper on my first time out for a real meal in more than a month. I indulged as I do whenever someone else is picking up the tab. We had appetizers and big entrees along with four or five beers, and I felt well-fortified for the meeting that I assumed would be short and pointless.

It was pointless, but it was not short. For starters, the meeting did not start right when I came up to the office. I had to help everyone with our spreadsheets, which doesn't mix well with a buzz. Ellen could tell I was exasperated, but she watched as Mary Jane and I and the others completed the numbers. We finally started the meeting itself at around 6:30. Under Ellen's direction, we "brainstormed about how we can turn this office into the most political office anywhere" and then decided who would "bottom-line" each task. Of course, nobody ever mentioned anything we talked about.

It was a waste of time, but it still wasn't the last of this. Ellen told us we were expected to take part in a conference call at 9 p.m. We each had to write down fifteen friends' names that we could call to tell them about Progressive Futures and let them know we were hiring. The conference call was to instruct us on how to do this. The five directors from our office were part of a group of exhausted and annoyed people who gave a dreary "Here" when the recruitment person took attendance. She then proceeded to walk through a sample phone call to a friend so that we would know what to expect when we spoke to our own friends.

I called a few of my friends and felt like a boob for talking about PFI with people I ought to have been catching up with after not speaking for so long. One of my friends had a father who was dying of cancer, and instead of checking in with him on his father's health, I was calling him to try to recruit him. Fortunately, most of my friends were busy and didn't pick up their phones late on a Sunday night. Eddie was in a bar somewhere and couldn't hear a word I said. I sent him a text telling him not to worry about it; then I grumbled the results of my outreach efforts at 10 p.m. when I called them in.

It was an insane day. Pointless activities send me into a rage, especially when they proceed on a schedule that I cannot anticipate. I had already worked over seventy hours that week, and I believed I had a right to a restful Sunday. Instead, I had been maneuvered into a day of work.

I never thought about quitting, though. As ticked-off and overtired as I was, I found new inspiration on the Metro ride back that night. I overheard an exchange among four teens and a guy who was reading the Bible. Although the teenagers were dressed like the rebellious ones who brood in the far back corner of the class, they were brimming with enthusiasm for the Bible. They told the man they were in town with their church to march in a protest against *Roe V. Wade* and gave him a brochure with the date and time. It made me want to vomit. These people had prospered in Washington for the past eight years, and it was time for them to go. I vowed once more to do everything I could.

The yellow line train runs on an elevated track above the Potomac, so I peered out at the Washington Monument as we passed over the river. Two red plane lights on top seemed to be flashing at me. I looked around the train and I saw that nobody else noticed them.

Chapter 12

From Song of the Broad Axe

The main shapes arise!
Shapes of Democracy total, result of centuries,
Shapes of turbulent manly cities,
Shapes of the friends and home-givers of the whole earth,
Shapes bracing the earth and braced with the whole earth.

-Walt Whitman

A man walked up to me. One minute later, he was $500 poorer.

I was canvassing by a bust of George Washington next to the Foggy Bottom Metro station on the GW campus. It was already three o'clock, and it had been a rough day. Streams of people had passed. The crowd seemed to consist of surly hospital employees, bored summer undergrads, and scrupulous State Department staffers. I had too much competition for their attention. There was a hot dog stand, an Obama paraphernalia stand, and a couple of guys selling flowers and playing an R&B station out of an old boombox. They turned far more heads than I did.

The pressure didn't get to me. I fed off the traffic that kept going by, knowing that the law of averages would have to prevail. As long as people were walking by, I would have a chance to raise money.

I started focusing my attention in on a particular person out of a crowd. I would make eye contact with that one person and ask that person if he or she had a minute for the Democrats instead of asking everyone who walked by at once. If you ask a passing group a question without addressing anyone, everyone in the group believes he or she has the right not to answer you. But if you ask one person a question, he or she feels obligated to answer. Such were the hard-earned lessons of Foggy Bottom, and I was determined to learn them regardless of the toil they required.

The approach paid off. I asked one person if he had a minute for the Democrats, to which he shook his head. I told him to have a great day and began looking to see who was coming next. Just then, I noticed a man who had passed coming back over. He nodded when I asked him if he had a minute for the Democrats.

He nodded again as I delivered my rap and, when I asked him whether he could support us today, he told me that he had been meaning to do this. I handed over the clipboard to let him write out his information, and I saw he wrote "Physician" in the occupation box of the form, so I asked him if he could donate $270 for the 270 electoral votes Barack Obama would need to elected President on November 4th. He stopped writing.

"I'm going to give you $500," he said. Then he went back to writing. A few moments later, he walked away with his pink tear-off receipt like it was a regular purchase. That was my first $500 donation.

Not everyone was as supportive. I was assigned to Friendship Heights the next day, and it did not live up to its name. Friendship Heights is a shopping area. It's the only place I've ever seen a Polo store next to a Barney's of New York next to a Cartier Diamonds next to a Coach next to a Louis Vitton. You would think people with such wealth would be jolly, but you would be wrong. It is another place that canvassing groups have hit up too many times for too long.

The day I went to Friendship Heights, I was showing a new director the ropes on her first day. Tia was a prim recent college grad who didn't seem so sure about canvassing. The first person who stopped to talk with us was a pleasant-looking older woman who smiled when we asked if she had a minute for the Democrats. Tia launched into her first rap, but the woman cut her off.

"You've got a lot of nerve," she told Tia. "My sister was raped by a black man and my mother was killed by a black man. And a black man will be in the White House over my dead body." Then the woman turned and walked away. I was shocked that a passerby could say something like this to a stranger. Tia was more thick-skinned than I would have been on my first day and showed no ill effects of the venom this woman spat at us. We managed to scrape together a decent day. On the other side of the street from us, another canvasser didn't raise a dollar the entire day. A woman had told him in the morning that he was doing a terrible job, and he never recovered.

I had a similar experience the next day on Connecticut and K, where I was unprepared for the crowds. I hadn't canvassed downtown much, and I had not yet figured out the fine art of trimming an overwrought rap into a pithy spiel. Most people ignored me on their way to lunch or the Metro, and nobody had the time to chat. Finally, late in the day, I found an audience. A middle-aged white guy with short black hair and sunglasses listened to my whole rap in a patient manner. He seemed interested in giving, and he asked me why I was out here. I answered with my go-to answer at the time, my argument that the gathering of small donations would give people a personal investment in this election and make the party more accountable to the small donor instead of the person who could slap down $28,500 at the drop of a hat.

"I'll tell you what," he said. "I've worked hard my entire life for what I have, and I support a wife and two kids with the money I make. When the government takes my money away from me, I think that amounts to socialism." I looked at him in silence, not sure how to react. He kept talking.

"I'll tell you something else. I could have dropped down $20,000, so that's how wrong you had me pegged." He walked off with a smug grin at the idea that he had told me off. I could see him at dinner that night with his family, telling his wife and two kids that he had flustered me using his words and his wit. I'm sure they had a laugh. I wonder if they thought of me on election night or if they would remember me now. In a non-election year, they might be persuaded that the summer is too hot and the labor of life too tedious to give ill will to a stranger.

Such interactions bothered me. I only brought back $20 that day, and that guy might be satisfied to know that he had a lot to do with it. I still had difficulty getting my head around the idea that a stranger felt the need to mock me. It would take several more weeks before I put these people in the right perspective. I didn't know yet that they were a waste of my precious time, that I needed to be available for likely contributors. I also did not yet comprehend how canvassing, like life, involves a confluence of a thousand coincidences. I could exercise no control over most of them. These factors include the time of day, the weather, the mood of the passersby, their thoughts, their experiences, the day of the week, the logistics of the neighborhood, and others. I could fill up pages and pages listing the bizarre coincidences upon which canvassing depends. It was a long time before I realized that these people's reactions to me had more to do with their quiddities than with defects in my personality or character. They said what they did not out of personal spite, but rather because uncontrollable factors compelled them to do so. It's similar to the unrequited lover who feels that every action of the person he or she desires but cannot have is calculated to belittle or vanquish him, when, in reality, the desired person is acting on impulses wholly foreign to the lover. And the people who went out of their way to heap abuse on me can go to hell.

That, fortunately, is out of my control as well. If I had any say, though, some space in hell might be reserved for the former Hillary Clinton supporters who berated me and my colleagues that summer. These people identified themselves right away. "I was a Hillary supporter," they would begin. I would let out an inaudible sigh and think, "Here we go again." To the defeated Hillary proponents, the Democratic nomination had not been won by Barack Obama. He and the rest of the party, including me in my capacity as a canvasser for the DNC, had stolen it from her. It was Hillary's turn, they would say. Everyone had agreed about that and then you guys had to do this to her. They would point a menacing finger at me. Well, I'll tell you what I'm going to do, they would say. I'm going to vote for McCain and so is the rest of my family.

In this manner, these Hillary supporters employed the common tactic of so many Americans who speak of their right to vote as if it were a dagger to stick in the hearts of their political enemies. It's pure nonsense. Most people's threats are mere trifles. Talking about an action is the furthest opposite from doing it, and the human mind can change in split seconds. Even if these people did intend to vote for McCain in August, they would, in all likelihood, think differently of the matter in November. Theirs was a tired and galling approach, so I figured out the best way to respond. I knew that none of these people had any interest in making a donation, so I just made them feel uncomfortable for trying to vent their frustration with me. I feigned surprise at their words. I acted unacquainted with the notion that any Democrat might vote against the party. My eyes would take on the downcast look of an idealist who has had his hopes for a progressive future dashed. People who had been ready to tear me a new one would lose their malicious attitudes and slink away.

I wish I could have tried this on the day when a group of deranged former Hillary supporters showed up to tape a canvassing team outside our office. Three people drove up in a white conversion van and pointed a video camera at our canvassers. When one of the directors questioned them, they began shouting about how we would get what we deserved for what we did to Hillary. The three identified themselves as members of a group called Party Unity My Ass (PUMA) and guaranteed that we would lose the election. I don't know if these people were actually Republicans trying to sow discontent or whether this was a bona fide group, but these three people must not have accomplished whatever it was they were after. We never heard from them again.

It was not our office's last brush with the media, however. The following day, a novice canvasser had the misfortune of showing up at the house of a reporter for the Chicago *Sun-Times*. She got out her camera and had him perform the rap before peppering him with questions as though he were the White House press secretary, asking who he was working for, how much he was paid, and what his thoughts were on this or that. The reporter posted the video on the *Politico* website, and the world could see a stammering canvasser answering these multitudinous questions. By the end of the tape, it was obvious that this canvasser was not a cunning operative to be feared, but rather just a guy trying to make a buck working for a good cause.

Vern Phillips was satisfied with the guy's performance, but he was very concerned with the attention we had been receiving. He told us we shouldn't let our picture be taken by anyone, and that we needed to do our best to keep everyone on our staff from taking part in escalating arguments. He instructed us to train our canvassers on dealing with pushy people so that everyone knew how to diffuse these things before they turned into ugly publicity. Also, he forbade us from talking with our staff about PUMA or from conducting any trainings outside the office for the time being. That directive turned the office into a sweaty, crowded place where nobody could hear themselves think, but it was in our best interest to avoid the PUMA people. One of the more perceptive canvassers once took me aside to ask me what we would be telling everyone about the camera incidents.

"What camera incidents?" I asked him.

"Oh, gotcha."

Not all the publicity was bad. Our office was invited to hear DC Delegate Eleanor Holmes Norton speak at an event put on by the Democratic Youth Leadership Committee at a bar on U Street. That neighborhood was an appropriate setting. I walked over to the place with a new canvasser, an older black guy named Reggie Carrollton. He had worked at a burger joint on U Street many years ago, and he told me what it looked like when it burned on the terrible night of Martin Luther King's assassination in 1968. It had to be gratifying to him or anyone else who had witnessed the MLK riots to see young people of all colors celebrating the campaign of the first black president on the same street on election night forty years later. Reggie had seen a lot in his life. He was a Vietnam vet with scars on his face from a wound he got there, and he talked a lot about his loving and successful wife and children. We sat at the bar that day and talked about how good a drink tastes after a long day. When the organizers of the event put out the food, we jumped up first to help ourselves at his urging. And, many times after that day, he would grab me on the bicep with his still strong hands and ask, "Say, you remember that time we got to that food first?"

He had love and joy to share, and he did so with everyone in the office. There was not one person he couldn't make friends with, and people on the street could feel the love he had for them too. Anytime a black woman walked by, he would say, "That's a Michelle Obama smile I see there. Come on now, you know we've got to talk!" One time an Iraq veteran gave Reggie his dogtags because he was overcome with the sight of old veteran on the streets working to end the war.

He took me aside another day to tell me that he was dying of cancer. I didn't ask for details, but he said he didn't have long to go. I could see him struggling to keep up with the young people, but he refused to take it easy. "I've got to do this," he would say. "I got to make it to Election Day."

The event we attended on U Street that night marked the beginning of a new website called runacampaign.org, which encourages young progressives to run for political office by giving them advice and resources to start a campaign. One of the organizers spoke of the need for a "Democratic Heritage Foundation" to provide the party with a steady stream of young progressives with the discipline and intellectual vigor to lead in politics. Norton admired the work our office was doing and she was inspiring in asking us to stay involved with the Democratic party.

The organizers also showed a film of party dignitaries urging us to run for office. It sounded plausible until Howard Dean came on. The man for whom we were raising money day and night read a teleprompter. His dullness on tape cast a pall over the event, which was otherwise pleasant. Our staff joined a large group of young people who cared enough to show up, and we shared stories. It motivated me to think that young people could be a big factor in the election.

I carried that sense with me in canvassing, reaching a new milestone the next day. I stopped sixty people for the first time while I was canvassing in Tenleytown. Before that day, forty stops was a good total for me, but sixty soon became the norm. I referred to a sixty-stop day as a "Sammy Sosa" level of stops, and I expected it of myself every day. The transformation was a key to my development as a canvasser. My mind found a link to my days as a teenager at Kauffman Stadium in Kansas City. Eddie and I attended about seventy games a year, and we arrived early for a chance to talk to somebody important. We would stake out a place near the entrance to the home team dugout and get the attention of everyone who came in from the field. We were only after a little acknowledgment. We never expected any of the players or team dignitaries to stop and talk to us, but we did expect them to smile and wave, acknowledging that we were great fans for being there every day and great people to support such a bad team.

I wanted everyone around to react to me, and I transferred it to my canvassing. I stood by a Robeks smoothie shop in Tenleytown, not far from American University, and I spoke to everyone who passed. I no longer tried to judge passersby before they spoke to me. I didn't care if it was a student listening to an iPod or a group of colleagues on their lunch breaks. They had to tell me whether they had a minute for the Democrats. I looked people right in the eye to make sure they knew I was speaking to them, and let them respond to me. And I mastered so-called "second grabs," which is how you respond to people who give you a stock excuse. Many people are ambivalent about stopping. They mutter something non-committal and keep walking. I began to shrug at them and discovered that people feel obligated to make themselves understood. When I acted as though I didn't hear them, people felt compelled to make me understand what they had said. Their effort was another opportunity to ask for money, and it often worked.

I was having a great time out there in Tenleytown when I paused to get a phone call I won't soon forget. I carried my phone at all times, but it was sometimes difficult to hear with cars going by, and I refused to interrupt conversations with possible donors. This time, though, I heard the ring and wasn't talking to anybody.

"Hi, this is Albertine O'Connell," the voice said. "You called me a couple of days ago after my interview in your office."

"Oh, yeah," I said. "How are you?"

"I'm good. I'm sorry I didn't return your call before. I'm in the process of moving to DC. I'll be there next week. I just need to decide between Progressive Futures and another group that's offering me a job."

"What group is that, if you don't mind my asking?"

"It's Greenpeace." I almost gagged. All of us hated Greenpeace because of the way their canvassers gave other groups' canvassers a bad name by being obnoxious. Instead of asking people if they had a minute for the environment, or something harmless and polite, they would ask people if they cared about the environment, or if they wanted to save the planet, or another iteration of a self-righteous question like that, and then they would walk alongside people to convince them to stop. I considered their practices unprofessional. I figured I'd try another tack with Albertine.

"Greenpeace is a great group," I said. "And the environment is a huge issue. But it's also a huge issue in this election, and if you came and worked for us, you'd have a real chance to make an impact on this election. We're in a great place to be talking politics with people, and we've got a great group in the office right now. I really think you'd like being a part of the team, but, you know, it's like you said, you've got a choice to make and it's up to you."

She laughed. "Well, I have been leaning towards Progressive Futures."

"That's terrific. You know, you should come in for a day at least, just see what you think of the office and what we do. At the end of the day, if it's not for you, there's no harm done."

"Yea," she said. "I can do that." We agreed on a date for her to come in and hung up. In the course of our relationship, of which I still had no inkling or hope, it would be far from the last time that Albertine disguised her true feelings from me.

Nobody would have wanted to work for Greenpeace in the middle of an election. The notion that she was weighing our office against that group was pure fancy, communicated for the purpose of making me demonstrate how much I wanted her to come work for us. Without thinking about it, for the first time, I had gone above and beyond to convince her to give up a fictitious non-committal stance either because my mind was dulled by ecstatic exertion or because love makes a fool of me more readily than anyone else in the world. I had no idea of this at that time, of course, excepting the part about love making a fool of me. I just remembered that she was attractive and that I wanted more attractive women in the office. No other thoughts about her occurred to me that day.

I was absorbed in badgering the fine people I met. The more I threw myself out there, the more people responded. They saw my sweaty, sunburned face as a human who deserved their attention for fighting for something they believed in, and they told me so by listening to me. I realized that the ill will I received ran in an inverse proportion to the degree to which I asserted myself. When I muttered my line in a tone calculated not to bother anybody, the only people who had time for me were the ones who wanted to cut me down. After that day in Tenleytown, I didn't care what people thought of me in public. I got into the election to make a difference, not to safeguard my dignity. I felt once again the joy of labor. And everyone told me the sun I got that day looked good on me, too.

Chapter 13

From Inebriate of Air

Inebriate of air am I,
And debauchee of dew,
Reeling, through endless summer days,
From inns of molten blue.

-Emily Dickinson

Canvassing also resembles life in that the elation of it cannot last. Each day is a new fight where the people you speak to display peculiarities that make this day different from the one before. I may have felt I owned the streets of Tenleytown on Monday, August 18th, but Tuesday was the opposite feeling.

I was standing downtown in the sun to show World Bank employees and others how dedicated I was, but most assumed I was a fool. A woman thought she was being helpful to me when she stopped and asked,

"Do you know where you are? You're in Washington, D.C. ,next to the World Bank. Everyone here is going to vote Democratic or can't vote because they aren't citizens. You should be in Virginia."

Before I could tell her that I was here to raise money so that the party could go to Virginia, and that I had been to Virginia several times, and that I could tell her more about the significance of Virginia to this election than she might have cared to hear, she sighed and walked away.

An Indian man thought he was being insightful when he shushed me by raising his finger and poking at the DNC letters on my clipboard. He wagged his finger at me and shook his head.

"Vy must people give money to dis group instead of candidate himself? Dis is codduption." He put his hand up to shut me up again and walked away before I could tell him that what I was doing makes the party more transparent, and that I had taken a class in college about campaign finance and I was well aware of corruption and the appearance thereof, and that my efforts constituted neither.

Another woman thought she was being sympathetic when she compared me to a homeless person. She said she didn't have a minute, then she got in her car and watched as someone waved me off like a pest. That's when she rolled down her window and remarked, "It's like being a homeless person, huh?" She drove away before I could reply.

There was a kernel of truth in her question, though. Canvassing is similar to panhandling in a lot of ways, though it might be considered professional panhandling. The effective panhandler, just like the effective canvasser, makes it clear why he or she needs money and tells everyone to have a good day. At 18th and I, I felt a different connection with the homeless.

Late in that afternoon, a schizophrenic came lumbering down the street. His face was scorched red and covered with overgrown facial hair. He was wearing old black sweatpants and he had a black sweatshirt on one side of his upper torso. He limped in his bare feet and he was screaming out, "Cocksucker! Motherfucker!"

It's been said that mentally disturbed people wear their souls inside out. At that time, this schizophrenic was my soul. There's a mad man inside me that I believe is inside every one of us. It's the part of me that yearns to violate every social norm by screaming at passersby what I think of them. I believe everyone has moments like this, but we have the ability to channel these impulses in ways that are useful or destructive.

On the corner of 18th and I, I realized that my life has been the result of the choices I've made in satisfying my various yearnings. Every one of my actions is the outward expression of a voice in my head crying at the top of its lungs to do something, do something now, do something today to satisfy my wishes either to accomplish something or to win the approval of others. My success has been the degree to which I can restrain myself towards a long-term goal in the monotony of a disciplined daily existence.

When the desires of electing Democrats and winning affirmation from others intersected that day, I felt the friction of two long-term goals not being met at once. I didn't tell anyone, though. I just smiled and told passersby to have a nice day. Then I went back to the office and conducted interviews as though nothing had happened.

The process of picking a vice presidential nominee can also be maddening. Dr. Hunter S. Thompson convinced me that the choice of Senator Thomas Eagleton doomed McGovern's insurgency candidacy in 1972. I was worried that Obama's decision might harm his chances. Since nobody votes for the vice presidential nominee, a presidential candidate should weigh the potential small improvements a possible veep might make to the ticket against that potential nominee's chances of losing the election for both of them.

Though some considered Dr. Thompson mad, I found his counsel very useful here. In his expert examination of the political football game of 1972, HST elucidated the veep nomination process to me. His teachings were particularly apropos in that McGovern had defeated the party establishment's choice in Humphrey just as Obama had defeated the party establishment's choice in Clinton. It was therefore necessary in 2008, just like in 1972, to find a running mate who answered a weakness about the candidate while satisfying the defeated establishment of the party. Dr. Thompson taught me how to interpret news coverage about the veep choice as well. The process of making the choice public starts with the whispers of leaks to the press gaggle which then conducts initial market research by publishing stories and eliciting reaction. If the pontificators give their thumbs up, the announcement becomes official.

Joe Biden's name was floated all over. The talking heads agreed that he balanced Obama's inexperience well, and the Scranton boy had been in Washington long enough to gain the establishment's favor. I didn't need the text message that the campaign sent out at 4 a.m. the Saturday before the convention to know that Biden would be tapped.

I now believe you can predict the outcomes of the American political process in the same way that I once ate psylocibin mushrooms and stuck my ear to the asphalt to listen for approaching cars. The murmurs start, and the perception that such and such bill will be passed or so and so should be appointed begins to build up in the same way that you can hear the faint purr of approaching cars. Perception equals reality with such frequency that the course of events can become easy to predict. In doing so, it is useful to remember that you don't have to press your ear to the middle of the road to know that cars are coming.

I wasn't making any guarantees about the election at that point, though. The polls were a statistical tie, and the thought of John McCain as our next president was plausible. For that reason, I had nothing cocky to say when I met a Republican National Committee fundraiser through a mutual friend that Saturday night in Adams Morgan. He didn't do any street canvassing, of course, but it was amusing to swap money-badgering stories. I was amiable enough to not comment on how divorced from reality he was to remark that a McCain-Romney ticket would be unstoppable. He had been a Romney staffer, and the news that his candidate had turned off voters all over the nation during the primaries would have been tough for him to bear. I did send him into conniptions when I set the stage for Obama's upcoming speech at Mile High by asking him to visualize that stadium filled to the brim with people of all races to cheer on the charismatic first black nominee for president on the anniversary of the "I have a dream" speech. I felt good enough about our chances to paint this image for him, but not good enough to be sanguine about the election.

The Democratic convention began the following Monday. Hillary Clinton made the most memorable speech of the first three days. Her supporters had threatened bloody murder in the form of electoral stakes in my heart if she were not chosen as the veep nominee, but they would have been better served with their ears to the asphalt. There was no logic in choosing someone who would weigh down the ticket. The point of the primary was that Obama's vision of a new, bold, left-leaning direction had beaten out a return to the Clinton trigonometry of the third way. Hillary Clinton's selection would have nullified that victory. I love Hillary Clinton as much as any of her supporters because the woman had the audacity to say that she would "strongly consider" choosing Obama as her running mate when she was behind in the primaries, and I love anyone with that kind of gall. But 2008 was not, and never was, "her turn."

To her credit, Hillary showed class and grace in her convention speech. Her still-inflamed supporters had wagged their fingers at me and declared that they would bolt the party if her excellent campaign was not recognized and if she did not play a prominent role in the convention. She achieved both with a meaningless delegate-counting exhibition on the floor of the convention and the headline speech on Tuesday night. She gave her full support to Obama. Hillary's speech also coined a phrase that I keep with me to this day, that of "keep going." This section of the speech invoked a famous saying of Sojourner Truth's on the Underground Railroad. In another moment that illustrates why I will always admire Hillary, she had the self-righteousness to compare the Democrats' struggles in 2008 with that of runaway slaves. The arena was packed with people of every heritage, and she insulted everyone's ancestors in one fell swoop when she said, "If you feel like they're gaining on you, keep going! If you feel like slowing down, keep going! If you feel like stopping, keep going!" The crowd exploded into cheers and I exploded into laughter.

I never thought of quitting. This election had saturated my mind to the point that I thought of nothing else, so any other course of action did not occur to me. My friend Sara was not so lucky. Sara was another director whose wonderful accent betrayed her New York Jewish heritage, and she was a spitfire who gave it back to every one who harassed her on the street. She downed coffee and diet Cokes all day, and never stopped. Sara and her friends from George Washington University enjoyed my company for who I was, and they flattered me by their presence. Progressive Futures wasn't for her, though. Sara had disliked canvassing and the pressures of being a director. The thought of two more months of it appalled her, so she quit the day after Hillary's speech.

Her resignation had implications for my own status. It was apparently the policy of Progressive Futures that the DNC offices would be steered by two directors in the fall. Adam Jacobs called me to ask me to be one of the two for the DC office. My new title would be "lead assistant director," so Adam billed it as a promotion. There was, of course, no raise. Adam told me over the phone that this was my chance "to work directly for the party" and to "get on the frontlines in Virginia." I knew he framed the job this way because someone, probably Ellen, told him that I knew politics and he wanted to win me over by making a political appeal. The realization annoyed me in the first place because the guy thought he knew how to convince me of something when he didn't really know me, and in the second place because it was an express, legal fact that working for PFI was not working "directly for the party." I agreed to become lead assistant director in the end because he reminded me that a new PFI assignment would mean that I would be responsible for finding housing again. I knew I would never find a setup like I had at Stan and Jenny's and, when I had confirmed that I could stay at their home until the end of the election, I told Adam it was a go. I had won the privilege of witnessing this election in our nation's capital.

I was filled with expectations for the next two months. Ellen was a cause for concern, though. I loved her like a big sister one day and hated her like an enemy the next. Since I knew Ellen's support was the only political leverage I had with Progressive Futures, I stayed on her good side by doing what she asked without talking back. But she was a hard person to work for.

Some days she could be so helpful. One day, she taught me a phrase that turned me into a better canvasser overnight, "right now." When I told her how a woman had just turned me down in favor of going online, she showed me how she nodded her head at people, looked them in their eyes, and said, "You should just give right now." This was especially useful to a person with eyes like Ellen's. It wasn't an argument based on reason or inspiration. Rather, it was simple peer pressure. Canvassing is based on uncomfortable exchanges and people feel strange talking to someone on the street. They feel intimidated by the dedication of the canvasser, and want to say or do something to justify themselves. So they say they will give online to end the conversation in a way that they think will appease us. Most people who say this have no intention of giving online, but a few are being honest. The game then becomes convincing those few to give right now instead of online, and the canvasser can go about this in two ways: rationality or pressure. I would master the rationality route in a couple of weeks, but Ellen taught me pressure, which is probably more difficult to master. When she implored people to give "right now" by telling them to do so in stark terms, she made it clear to the people who feel awkward enough to do anything to appease us that they couldn't do so without making a contribution.

The effect was remarkable. One time, there was a guy walking away from a Whole Foods with two heavy bags of groceries who promised he would make a donation online. I just looked at him in his eyes, shrugged my shoulders, and said, "Ah, you should just give right now," as if it were a matter of convenience. The guy put down his bags and made a $25 donation. There was a couple going out for brunch who wanted to have a nice day and think about something else and give online later. I made the same shrugging gesture and said, "Nah, you should just give right now." There was a moment of silence, and the guy said a simple "Sure." He donated $100.

It was incredible to me that people could be convinced not by logical argument, but by the feeling that I communicated when I acted as if they were lame. When someone tells you to do something, you have to make a choice between obeying and disobeying. I was standing in the hot sun with an earnest smile and telling people how much we had to do to win this election, how they had to do their duty. By saying no to a "right now" request, they would be doing a disservice. When I shrugged and advised them to give today, I was in effect saying, "C'mon, don't be lame. Reward my hard work" without saying anything of the kind. These kind of subtle pushes to give right now are essential to effective canvassing. To take advantage of them, I had to tell people what they should do. I didn't realize I could do so until Ellen showed me that.

She was also harmful to my canvassing on some days. I canvassed with her in Silver Spring, and she requested that I canvass right next to her. We stood face to face outside of a Borders Books. She started out the day strong with a couple of $100 donations and began to drill me. Every time a person approached, she whispered for me to shake their hands, to introduce myself, to get their attention earlier, to use the response structure, to smile more broadly like she was. Then she would motion for me to come over and speak with her, and she would tell me how people wouldn't respond to my intensity and I needed to dial it down and not try so hard. She made me feel like she thought I had no idea what I was doing. I had been canvassing for about six weeks and I was getting better every day, so I don't know why she thought she had to treat me like this. My confidence had been on a high from four straight days over $200, but she shattered it in front of Borders. I made $15 all day, and, by the end of the day, I no longer had any composure left.

I took Ellen aside before leaving the office that night. I wanted to understand why she thought I needed so much attention out there.

"Oh, I just thought you weren't doing well, so I wanted to help you," Ellen said. "I just said anything that came into my head. You shouldn't take any of it seriously." I was too stunned to say anything, so I said good night and went home wondering how someone who was around me as much she was could be so oblivious of my feelings. I hated her the way I've hated everyone in my life who puts a dent in my enthusiasm.

There were a lot of those times. Anytime Ellen was in the room when I spoke to someone, whether it was a canvasser, an interviewee, a phone caller, Ellen would hover around and correct me. "Schedule them for today!" she would whisper in my ear while I talked to the job applicant. "Make sure you get everyone practicing soon," she said from the computer while I was training canvassers one morning. It was exasperating, but I never told her once how I felt because I knew a negative word from her could send me to a random PFI office on the other side of the nation.

Then there were times when I was glad I let her walk all over me because I loved her. We watched Obama's speech from Mile High Stadium at an event for the Arlington Young Democrats. When Sen. Dick Durbin introduced his colleague by saying, "He inspires young organizers in canvassing offices to work day and night for him," Ellen and I looked at each other through tears. We shared camaraderie at that moment not just in that what Durbin said described us, but also because we each could tell the other was so dedicated to this cause that Dick Durbin could make us cry.

We did have a great time together that night. She told me about Jean-Pierre's latest exploits in France and talked about how she had been fitted to wear her mother's wedding dress. She also told me how much she appreciated my hard work. I told her the truth, that it was a pleasure to work among intelligent women.

There was another intelligent woman at that convention-watching party: Albertine O'Connell. She had come with some friends, and she chatted with us before rejoining them at another table. I can't recall the few words we exchanged. I am thankful that no soothsayer came and tapped me on the shoulder to tell me that this woman would become the first woman to give me the time of day in less than a month because I know I would have done something to prevent it. If I had known the significance that the woman who I figured was unattainable at that time would have for me, I would bet John McCain's seven houses that I would have marched up to her friends and communicated my peculiarities in some way or another that would have altered our fates. Luckily, there are no soothsayers in Arlington. It was better to be surprised anyways.

But I'll never forget Obama's speech from that night. It wasn't so much the content itself, which resembled his stump speech. It was the crowd. There was a mass of people of all ages and backgrounds filling every seat and square foot of the stadium to cheer on a man they all believed in. My favorite moment was after the speech, when they played "Signed, Sealed, Delivered," and the camera panned over the stadium to show joyous people dancing together, with everyone in attendance believing that this man could change the country the same way they believed in the love that brought them together. They didn't want to leave the stadium to beat traffic, they wanted to savor the night and each other. I wanted that moment to last forever, but I won't forget that image.

The crowd made me think of my parents and all the boomers who wanted to change the world back in the Sixties. I had this feeling that I was trying to satisfy those ambitions. Here was a chance to show that America is a place where you can help your neighbors without calling them welfare queens and where you can end wars without losing them. Obama made this idea possible once again to Sixties liberals who had felt betrayed for so long. I was trying to make my parents' dreams come true.

I had to call them. My dad answered, but he said my mom was upstairs getting ready for bed.

"No need to wake her," I said.

"Nonsense, Toby," he said. "She'll want to talk to you. Hold on a second. Emma! Emma! No, everything's fine! It's Toby! He's called to talk about Obama's speech tonight! Grab the phone and make sure you hit the talk button!"

"Hi, Toby," I heard my mom's voice. "Thanks for calling. Did you see the speech?" I sighed.

"Of course I saw the speech, Mom," I said. "I called because it made me think of you guys."

"We were thinking of you, too, Toby," my dad said. "It was an amazing sight."

"Mom," I said. "It made me think about that time you read me the Langston Hughes poem where the mother tells her son that 'Life ain't no crystal stair.'"

"That's wonderful, Toby," she said. "But I don't remember reading you Langston Hughes. I thought we read you Frost or Kipling, but I never remember reading you that poem. When was that, do you know?"

"I don't recall, Mom," I said, a little disappointed by her reaction and unwilling to try to pinpoint a date. "I was pretty young."

"How young? You can't have been too young, because I wouldn't have tried reading a poem like that to you if you couldn't grasp it."

"I don't know, Mom. The point is that I thought of that, and I think of you guys a lot while I'm doing this. I know I used to make fun of you for talking about the Sixties all the time and living in the past and all that, but I think I've found my Sixties."

"We're amazed at what you're doing, Toby," my dad said. "We think of you every day and we wonder if this will actually happen."

That night stiffened my resolve. We had to win, I decided, or there wouldn't be a chance for idealism ever again.

Chapter 14

A Portrait of the Times

Two W.P.A. men
stood in the new
sluiceway

overlooking
the river—
one was pissing

while the other
showed
by his red

jagged face the
immemorial tragedy
of lack-love

while an old
squint-eyed woman
in a black

dress
and clutching
a bunch of

> late chrysanthemums
> to her
> fatted bosoms
>
> turned her back
> on them
> at the corner
>
> -William Carlos Williams

I got a new boss on Labor Day. Dan Blackledge became the new canvass director of the street team, and he bussed in that afternoon from New York to take over. Ellen didn't leave, though. She stayed in the office as the director of the door canvass, near enough to nag me whenever the rigors of directing became too much for her to bear alone.

But reporting directly to Dan would be a change. I heard through people who knew of him that he had moved up from canvasser in PFI's New York City office due to his astronomical canvassing average and tireless work ethic.

He came into the office carrying a two-gallon water bottle and a rolling suitcase. Dan had long, straight brown hair which he kept pushing out of his face, and the worn yellow dress shirt he was wearing was soaked in sweat. Instead of exchanging pleasantries, he reached for the binder where we kept the crew sheets, the records of each canvasser's daily totals, and plopped down in one of the ratty chairs to examine it. I pretended to be reading something on the computer, but I was watching him closely. He took out a blank bound book and started making notes with a pen he had propped behind his ear. Those books went everywhere with him. They looked like coffee table books but the covers were white with no writing on them and the pages were blank and unlined. Dan wrote in them every day. When he wasn't writing, he gnawed at the end of the pen in a way that I knew meant his mind was absorbed by everything except the pen. Dan looked up at me after a while.

"Have you guys been running a night canvass?" he asked me. I told him we had at some points during the summer, but had stopped recently due to reduced staff.

"We'll have to bring that back," he said. "It's painful for us, but it means more money." He went back to reading and writing for another half hour or so. Then he got up and showed me what he was working on.

"Take a look at this," he said, thrusting the book in front of my face. I looked down to see a page of doodles with "400,000" scrawled in the middle and circled. "If we do everything right, we can raise over $400,000."

I nodded and took him in one more time. I saw right then that he was one person who wanted to work harder than me and wanted me to work harder than I was working. His eyes and his scruffy, wet face communicated a lack of sleep and hygiene and a corresponding depth of commitment. It was inspiring and unsettling at once.

What was inspiring was how much money I began to raise in the wake of Obama's acceptance speech. I canvassed downtown near Metro Center at 13th and G on the Friday after the convention, and I had adjusted my rap to fit the demeanor of the prosperous professionals there. I spoke with more than sixty of them that day, and I brought back $515 from fourteen donations.

"It's been an inspiring week," I told everyone who stopped to listen to me. "But we can't forget all the work we have to do. We need to put more organizers on the ground, train more volunteers to get out the vote like never before, and get our message on the air. With only sixty-four days left, we need to do this right away. The great thing about our campaign is that, just like the Obama campaign, the DNC is going to fund its entire campaign through individual support. That means no contributions from special interest PACs or corporate lobbyists. And that's why I'm out here today." Then I would hand the clipboard over to the person. "Here's my statement of support. The best way to get involved is by making a donation today. We take all forms of payment, and these resources constitute the ground game that will turn this election into one that we'll never forget. Would you be able to support us today?"

I delivered this thirty-second speech with unsmiling conviction, and the response was overwhelming. I've never seen so many people ready to give right when I finished talking. The most frequent response was "Sure," though my largest donation was $100 a lawyer agreed to give on the spot. He wrote in his credit card info like it was part of the food court lunch he was holding in his other hand. Six weeks ago, he would have made my day, but on that day I realized that this type of donor was not the one I enjoyed finding the most. My favorite donor was an elderly black man in a walking cap who wrote down $35 in cash on the form and looked around nervously.

"Is there somewhere we can go so that we're not in the middle of the street?" he asked. I was confused and worried he was one of those people who didn't understand that the form meant that you would be giving money that day, but I didn't show it. I suggested we go inside a nearby ATM enclosure, and he agreed. When we got inside, he checked all directions again, and crouched down for his sock, from which he pulled out a small wad of bills. He peeled off $35 before wadding the rest up and returning it to his sock. Then I understood the personal danger this man was overcoming in making a donation, and I felt an ineffable gratitude to him.

It also indicated what I needed to do as a canvasser to succeed. I needed to look people in the eyes, tell them what they wanted to hear, and do anything necessary to get them to give right then and there. From that day on, I never hesitated to lead someone to a bench or an overhang or anywhere that would make them more comfortable. I never appeared desperate, never let it be seen that the thought that the fear of rejection was pounding in my brain. I just made it easy to give today. And it worked.

Soon people had more reasons to give. The Republican National Convention started the following week, and it was chock full of the brand of conservatism that made President Bush so unpopular, although he appeared only by video feed. The most disturbing aspect of the event was the crowd on the convention floor. Almost all of the delegates were white, and they seemed filled with hatred of the idea that Barack Hussein Obama could be our next president. Hate was evident in the chants of "Drill baby drill!" which were a great civic contribution to our nation's debate about how best to end our dependence on foreign oil; it pervaded the chants of "Zero! Zero!" that were a dignified expression of the question of whether Obama had any executive experience; and it seethed from the jeers that Sarah Palin and Rudy Giuliani drew by mocking Obama's experience as a community organizer.

It made me want to puke. The crowd embodied my enemies, the people holding this nation back. They are the reason that we've fallen behind the industrialized world in health care and education and infrastructure. These people have so little love for their neighbors that they believe that life is a competition and only the virtuous are winners. They are the reason that so much of our voting public believes that the most vote-worthy politician is the one who seems like he could have a beer with them. They are the people who believe that an individual's race and religion define that person's goodness. They are the reason that America has become a laughingstock in the eyes of the world and the cause of most of our country's problems.

That Republican National Convention crowd reminded me of a time at training. I was sharing my thoughts on becoming a director with Dan, and I told him I was excited to get involved, that this felt like a form of agitation, although, I said, "I know agitation is not what we're about." Dan looked at me for a second as if he were ensuring I was serious.

"It is agitation," he said. I knew he was right when I saw this crowd that represented everything that I want to change about America. It was invigorating to think I could do something about it.

Other people felt the same way. The day after Palin's speech, the Obama campaign received $8 million in donations from across the country. The polls after the conventions placed

McCain ahead of Obama for the first time, and it became even easier to raise money. For my purposes, the RNC gave birth to "Palin talking points" which I used every time someone said he or she would rather give online.

"I completely understand," I would say in an obliging voice. "It's very easy and convenient to give online. But I want you to give this way, on the street, in public, with all the connotations that apply. We're raising money in an unprecedented manner with no contributions from special interests or lobbyists in the most transparent method possible, and I want you to be a part of it. Furthermore, when you give this way, you're showing Sarah Palin and Rudy Giuliani that it is, in fact, our community organization that will win this election."

It didn't matter that this argument had nothing to do with the fact that many people are uncomfortable with sharing their credit card information with an obnoxious guy wielding a clipboard. People gave. I averaged $440 per day the week of the RNC, and $393 the week after. Everyone wanted to give, even some who told me upfront that they didn't want to make any donations. One woman saw me, told her friends she would catch up with them, and donated $250 without even listening to the rap. I won my second $500 contribution from a woman in the Clarendon shopping neighborhood of Arlington. She told me she had been a Hillary supporter, and hadn't known if she was going to support Obama. It was Palin that drove her back to the party.

When I was canvassing in D.C.'s Chinatown area, a British tourist wanted to give. I told him that noncitizens couldn't make any contributions, but he wanted to donate so much that he started asking everyone who stopped if he could give them cash to donate. I foresaw something damaging coming from this effort, so I took his money and made up a fake contributor form. It wasn't the first time I did this for someone, and it wouldn't be the last, either.

I don't know what the DNC did with invalid contributions like these, and I didn't care. I knew that if I were in charge there, I would have thrown the money in the pot with the rest because I disdain our campaign finance laws. I, like many liberals, used to admire John McCain for his role in the McCain-Feingold Act. Now I dislike him for it. It's not McCain's previous involvement in the Keating Five scandal, or the fact that most Republicans supported McCain-Feingold because it took soft money away from the Democrats, though political factors like these should be noted in any conversation about campaign finance. My objections come from the idea that such loophole closings are the means of eradicating corrupting influences in politics. The big donors will always find ways to give no matter what, so the emphasis shouldn't be on limiting their contributions. Disclosure is what's important. As long as the public knows who is financing which candidate or commercial, it doesn't strike me that anything corrupt is happening. The Swift Boat Veterans for Truth were a menacing presence in 2004 not because anyone believed that John Kerry did not actually serve with distinction in Vietnam, but rather because nobody could tell who was making these claims.

On top of that, canvassers should be able to be as successful as possible. I tried to explain this to a Feingold aide whom I spoke with in the Eastern Market one Saturday, that efforts like mine were everything we should reward in political work, not limit. She didn't seem interested in making shop talk on the weekend, though. I also ran into an aide for Sen. McCaskill that day. She donated $50, and we chatted about an opening for Staff Assistant I had heard about in the Senator's office. I told her that I hadn't had time to apply a few weeks ago when it came open, but I wished that I had.

"No, the work you're doing is far more important," she said. It was gratifying to hear that from a Hill staffer, and it fit with my sense of my job. Some days before, Ellen had asked me to put Progressive Futures posters up on the GW campus after a long day of work, and I was less than thrilled. I got as far as Washington Circle on the edge of campus before tossing them in a trashcan. I got on the Metro there and went home to rest for the next day, but I couldn't fall asleep. I couldn't stop thinking about those posters I had thrown away, those big pictures of Obama in the trash. I was worried that the trashed posters would be discovered. I had signed on to help make history, and I felt that I was involved in a meaningful way. If I got fired because Ellen or Vern Phillips happened to see posters sitting in the trash, I wouldn't be able to forgive myself. The next morning, I went back by Washington Circle and fished the posters out to take back to Stan and Jenny's where they would be safe. Campaigning felt like a privilege.

And sometimes it felt like an unbearable burden. My new status as lead assistant director meant that I would canvass only three days a week instead of the six that I had been accustomed to. The lost canvassing days would be made up with a multitude of administrative tasks, especially payroll. I had had no notion of payroll before Dan came because it was not in my realm. Sara had done payroll so well that nobody else needed to worry about it, but now it was my responsibility. It involved a massive Excel spreadsheet where every canvasser's daily totals needed to be recorded. It also required the entering of the personal information for all the new hires who came on during the two-week pay cycle. This sounds like a straightforward task, but complications came from the nature of the office. Our office accommodated more than fifty people who contributed trash, noise, and entropy all day. It was not a conducive environment for concentration or the keeping of vital papers. One missing crew sheet or I-9 form could throw the whole process off, and then our office's numbers would be askew and canvassers' pay would be affected.

I became aware of this by the second time I completed payroll, but the first time I did it was one of my toughest days at PFI. Dan had hinted that I would need to do payroll, but I had never seen the spreadsheet to know what that entailed, and he couldn't find the time to show me until the day before it was due to the national office. I spent eight hours that Saturday messing with the computer and scurrying around the office for missing documents. I finally completed it at around ten P.M. or so, and I was proud to report the news to Dan. Without saying thanks or even acknowledging that I had done anything, he sat down at the computer and found a bunch of mistakes.

All my life, the most galling moments have been times where I've thrown myself into a task for another person's satisfaction only to be met by a lack of appreciation. Usually, the person is too absorbed with the task at hand to be able to tell how hard I've worked or how much his or her gratitude would mean to me. At those times, I know my hurt feelings will not be edifying or helpful, so I leave. That's what I did Saturday night without losing my composure, and Dan was content to correct the damn thing himself. I sat on the stairs, exhausted. Then I took the train back to Arlington. I leaned my forehead against a cool metal pole and asked for the strength to make it to Election Night.

As I was walking back to Stan and Jenny's, Eddie called to ask if I wanted to watch the first Texas football game of the season that night. I had forgotten the Longhorns were playing. He said he was coming to pick me up, and I did my best to give him directions. He showed up twenty minutes later. In my haste to get ready, I forgot to see if Stan or Jenny was up to give me some directions to Georgetown, where Eddie said he had heard a lot of Texas alums would be watching the game at a bar. I also figured he would know how to get back to Georgetown based on the route he had taken to Stan and Jenny's.

I was wrong. We followed 395 across the water to get back into DC, and Eddie's mind seemed to be drawing a blank. When 395 ended, we found ourselves on Pennsylvania Avenue.

"Pennsylvania?" he said. "I like Pennsylvania. I can get to Georgetown from Pennsylvania."

"That's good," I said. "Because this doesn't look much like Georgetown." There were boarded-up windows in the shops by the side of the road, and the open ones offered payday loans and bail bonds. There were few, if any, people walking on the street, and the ones who were caused Eddie to roll up the windows and make sure the doors of his Taurus were locked. Fortunately for us, the one extravagance Eddie's parents didn't allow was a pricey car.

"Dammit," Eddie said. "It's so easy to get lost in this city. We must have just missed one turn. That's all you have to do here, and then there's no going back. I think I can find my way, though." Twenty minutes later, we were at the same intersection with the payday loans, or at least we thought it was the same one.

"OK," Eddie said. "I'm lost. No other way to put it. I have no idea where I am." We laughed for awhile, but it started getting old because we realized we were missing kickoff and probably some of the few interesting moments of the game. I could tell Eddie was starting to get tense, so I decided to have some fun with him.

"You getting scared yet, Eddie?"

"Huh?"

"Are you scared of this neighborhood?"

"You know what, man, yes, I am. There aren't a lot of people who look like me here. There are a lot of suspicious looking people walking around, and I don't know where I am. I'm going to be voting for a black guy to win the presidential election, but that has nothing to do with the fact that this is a strange neighborhood."

I activated my most patronizing tone. "Well, Eddie, if you think about it, neighborhoods like this aren't that strange. Every city in America has neighborhoods like this, whether you're comfortable with them or not."

"I know they do, Toby. I'm just saying that I would rather not find myself in one when I want to be in Georgetown watching the Longhorns." I decided it was a good time to bring up a class Eddie and I had taken about the treatment of minorities in our media. The professor was a large, opinionated, intelligent black woman, and I always thought Eddie felt threatened by such a woman talking to him about race.

"I wonder what Professor Willis would say," I said.

"I don't care what she would say, unless she knew how to get from Pennsylvania Avenue Southeast over to Georgetown. That's the only thing I'd like to hear from her right now."

"That figures. I bet she would have a lot to say about this situation."

"Well I don't give a fuck what she would have to say about this situation right now. I want to see the Longhorns play."

"Do you have a problem with a strong African-American woman, Eddie?"

"Dammit, I'm trying to figure out how to get to Georgetown and you keep bringing this shit up. It's not helping."

"Oh, but it's fun, though, Eddie. It's interesting."

"Yea, yea, you're right it is interesting. That was a good class, I learned a lot. But I wish you would shut the fuck up right now." Eddie pulled into a Wendy's to see if anybody could give us directions. I stepped out of the car well aware of the irony of asking how to get to Georgetown from Anacostia. The Wendy's was closed, but there was an employee locking up.

"Excuse me," I said. "Can you tell me how to get to Georgetown?"

"Como?" he answered.

"Usted sabe una manera para ir a Georgetown?" I figured he would at least understand my broken Spanish.

"Georgetown?" His face was blank. He had never heard of it. I thanked him and got back in the car. Eddie and I drove around an hour or so more and had a blast being lost until we finally found our way.

The next day, I found more inspiration to keep going. I had the day off, so I had planned to get some groceries. Unfortunately, my battery was dead. I didn't know what to do since Stan and Jenny were out of town, so I wandered over to their neighbor's garage, where I saw a man at work on his car. Tony was the guy's name, and I told him what was the matter. He dropped everything he was doing to help me. Tony knew a mechanic down the street, and he arranged for my car to get the best service. Then he gave me a ride to the service station while my Rav was getting towed. He bought cold drinks for the tow truck driver and me and saw to it that my car would be ready as soon as possible. On the way back, he took me by Giant so I could still get some groceries. When he dropped me back off at Stan and Jenny's, I thanked him with the profuseness that I thought was fitting. Tony just shrugged and said, "Ah, you would do the same for me if you could."

He was right. Tony was one of the thousands of people I met during the campaign. He wouldn't have been on the floor at the Republican convention, but he may not have been a Democrat, either. I don't know because we didn't talk politics. I worked harder for this election than I'd ever worked, harder than I knew I could, and I did it for Tony and everyone who made my time in D.C. special. And I did it because I love the people of this world and I hate war, poverty, and environmental degradation.

Chapter 15

A Drinking Song

Wine comes in at the mouth,
And love comes in at the eye.
That's all we shall know for truth
Before we grow old and die.
I lift the glass to my mouth,
I look at you, and I sigh.

-W. B. Yeats

Dupont comes alive at night. I used to walk down 20th Street just off the circle sometimes at the end of the day to meet up with friends for a beer or to ride home from the Farragut West station so I wouldn't have to transfer. The used book store, the copy place, and the old Brewmaster's Castle would be shut up for the night, but their floodlights and the street lights lit up some eye-popping evidence that I wasn't in Missourah.

One night, as I trudged down to the station, I saw two homeless men swinging giant tree branches at one another. They were screaming obscenities and bludgeoning each other. A cop car happened by. It came to a halt, and a massive officer jumped out. "What the fuck are you doing?" he yelled at them. He grabbed the branches from them and pushed them face down onto the pavement.

A couple was necking at the next corner. The movement of their hands on each other and the passion that made them unable to wait made me jealous and ecstatic at once.

A young mother pushed her baby home on a stroller. I looked her in the eyes and smiled.

I loved being part of this. In our tiny hovel of an office on the third floor, we toiled in this city of desperate, demanding people. It was exhausting, but I never wanted to be anywhere else.

Dan was one of these demanding people. As promised, he reinstituted the night canvass. This meant that a different crew of canvassers would come in to work from 1 to 9 p.m., and that I would need to stay until 10 or 10:30 to finish up. Dan informed me of this change one night when he approached me with his writing books to show me figures.

"Look at this," he said, opening the book to a page of doodlings and figurings. "A 'team' is six canvassers. Right now, we have, on average, 3.6 teams. I've done calculations that show that if we bring back the night canvass, we can be at 4.1 teams in one week, 4.9 the week after, and 5.5 the week after that. It's going to be painful, but we have to add another shift so we can hire more staff."

He was chubby and sweaty, his fifth cup of coffee for the day in one hand and a chewed-up pen in the other. Protest would have been pointless.

"We have about a month and a half to go before Election Day, and we don't know which way this thing is going to go. I want to rest after it ends, but I know I'm not going to be able to unless I feel like I did everything I could."

He was speaking my language. Dan deserved to run that office and call the shots because he worked the hardest. I'm not sure, but I think he lived there. Late one Saturday night, I made the mistake of trying to navigate D.C.'s highways and found myself near Dupont with no idea how to get back to Virginia. I parked next to the office to Google some kind of route back. The door to the office was the kind that requires jiggling, and I was fiddling with it when Dan suddenly swung it open.

His eyes were bloodshot and he was wearing the same clothes I saw him in earlier that day, a DNC shirt, a red bandana, and green pants with a stained seat. He looked like hell.

"What are you doing here?" he asked me. I told him without mentioning that I might wonder the same thing about him. He seemed satisfied with my answer and plopped down in one of the ratty office chairs.

"We can add a whole team next week," he said.

"Huh?" I looked away from the screen, not sure I heard him right.

"We can add a team next week. We need to hire fifty people, staff ten of them, and retain six of them. It's easy math."

"Mmmhmm," I replied. It was past midnight, and growing the office couldn't have been further from my mind. I wrote down the directions and got the hell out.

I didn't ask him where he lived because it was obvious that he didn't care. I don't think Dan did anything besides work. He was aware of life outside. We talked about Seinfeld episodes, LBJ, the election, politics as a whole, and David McCoullough's Truman biography, which he read once a year. But I could tell that nothing was more important than the office to him. Episodes like that Saturday night happened again and again, where everyone was ready to stop for the night, ready to grab a beer or chase a woman. Not Dan. All he wanted to do was calculate the office average, confirm that everyone would be canvassing tomorrow, and figure out ways to keep canvassers motivated.

As I've said, it was inspiring but disturbing. Humans are not constructed for work in all waking hours. Without some form of leisure, either the mind or the body will break down. Dan showed few signs of fatigue, though. He lived on coffee, cigarettes, donuts, and greasy hamburgers, and he devoted all his effort to the DC office of Progressive Futures Futures, Inc.

I never knew quite what to make of him, but I did my best for him. Everyone did, and we got results. Dan trained every canvasser to ask for the federal maximum contribution of $28,500 every time. It was a simple yet masterful tactic because it communicated the seriousness of this election and the seriousness of us as canvassers.

He also taught a shrewd bump-up tactic to turn $100 donations into $167 donations. Dan had found out that a Greyhound ticket from D.C. to Crawford, Texas, cost $167, so he had all of us asking for Dubya bus tickets. There were so many people who wanted to make $100 donations because it seemed like a reasonable figure for this historic election. We would thank them for the donation in a sincere, appreciative manner, then tell them about that bus ticket. Most of them couldn't resist putting down $67 more.

Americans celebrate people with the audacity to cut through euphemisms and ask a question point blank, and Washingtonians certainly responded to us. Our office had days of $8,000 raised, then $9,000, and weeks of $30,000 and $40,000. The canvasser average shot up well above $200, and the staff grew, though not at the extraordinary pace that Dan schemed in his books.

The place was a madhouse. That phone was ringing off the hook with people drawn by the ads we placed in the *Post* and Craigs list and the posters we put up on the college campuses. Every director in the office needed to answer these calls, schedule these people for interviews, describe how to get to our office, and hang up the phone to get the next caller on the schedule. Most days we had more than 100 calls, so it could be mind-numbing at times. It gave me a real understanding why old Bobby Seale referred to the telephone as "that damn bitch box." Because of the volume of calls, the voicemail on our phone was always full. Regional director Adam Jacobs at one time said this made our office "reek of inactivity." It was astonishing to me sometimes that Progressive Futures could have so many people on its staff that it didn't deserve and yet not even treat them with the proper respect. I was working fourteen hours a day and didn't have a second to worry about voicemail.

Dan instructed me not to use any evaluative process at all on the phones. We could pare down the ranks when they came for the interview, but we wanted to hire as many people as possible.

That made it necessary to get these calls over with as quickly as possible. "We pound the pavement. We talk to the people," I would tell callers. "We're a fundraising, canvassing office and we raise money all over this metropolitan area to elect Barack Obama and all the Democrats this fall. Does this sound like something that you'd be interested in?"

An affirmative answer meant an interview. The sessions were packed with people, and I introduced them to the office as fast as I could. Where before, I savored the info sessions as a form of oratory, I now kept them to ten minutes tops. Then we would hire people by the pack. It only took one sentence and one sizing-up to tell if someone could be a canvasser, so most individual interviews didn't last five minutes.

We also went directly to the campuses to find more employees. I chose Howard University, and I spent two days on that campus putting up posters, holding interviews, and hiring as many students as possible. I started out in the middle of the campus quad. First I got moved by a couple of fraternity guys who didn't want this goofy white boy standing on their frat's assigned part of the quad. They were polite enough not to put it that way. Then I moved to a spot on the sidewalk onto which all the paths converged and asked everyone who passed by if they wanted to help elect Barack Obama. That's when the campus police told me to take a hike, again not in so many words.

I resolved to get some lunch, so I ambled over to some food stands. I saw an item I had heard about it in a Lauryn Hill song but never seen: a beef patty on cocoa bread. It only cost a couple of bucks and it was delicious. It made me bilious, but it tasted great in the shade with an iced tea.

I've heard it said before that white people only gain rapport in a black neighborhood by not minding being the butt of jokes. I pride myself on my ability to laugh at myself, and I had plenty of opportunities to do so on those two days. A couple of guys walking up to class passed by me eating that spicy beef patty. They looked at me funny, but I just grinned.

"You look like Bill Gates," one of them said.

"Bill Gates? Nobody's ever told me that before."

"No, man. You're him. You look exactly like Bill Gates." The guy and his friends laughed some more and continued on to class. I had countless more interactions like that one in the afternoon and on the next day. I set up at a table outside the Starbucks on Florida Avenue, and I turned that table into my office. That's what I told people, too.

"Come on back at five o' clock," I'd say. "That's when I'll be holding the info session at my office."

"Where's that?" they'd ask.

"Right here, of course." Most people didn't know what to think. In my experience canvassing, most black people are far more interesting to speak with in daily life than white people. Many white people, especially middle-aged men, walk down the street with their hands in their pockets and take a wide berth around anyone who might try to speak to them. Sometimes these people don't respond at all when you ask them if they have a minute for the Democrats, but usually they just show you the palm of their hand and shoo you away like a mosquito. You get the feeling that you could ask them if they had a minute to keep you from raping their daughter, and they wouldn't pay you any mind, much less stop. As Malcolm X would say, you know how white people do.

Many African-Americans, on the other hand, are the opposite. They're not afraid to walk right next to another human being, not afraid to speak to another person, and not afraid to give you the dignity of a reaction. Black women in particular could sometimes put me in a positive mind just by the sheer love communicated by their quick conversation. "I'm sorry, baby," one might say. "I always got time for the Democrats, just not right now." I would smile, thank her for her support, and tell her to have a great day. "You do the same," she would say, and I just knew she meant it. These are the kind of conversations that kept me going, the kind when I could feel the love from people I didn't and couldn't know. I had them with people of all races and genders, and I had cold exchanges with people of all races and genders. To say otherwise would be rubbish.

I'm just saying, though, that people were animated on Florida Avenue those days, and it made me animated. I said my "pound the pavement" line again and again. People would shake their heads at me and say, "You're crazy."

"You got that right," I'd say. "I'm crazy about Barack Obama and all the Democrats. I'm out there." Then I'd gesture wildly like Kramer did on Seinfeld. I got a great response, hiring a dozen or so people over the two days, which was not bad considering we didn't do any preparation and I was just a guy jabbering at passersby outside of a Starbucks. One of the students I hired, a pretty freshman wearing a funky knit cap, told me I looked like John Lennon.

Only one person gave me ill will. She walked up to me with a crinkled brow and asked, "What you doin' out here?" in a threatening voice. I told her. She wagged her finger at me and pointed at the poster advertising for employment to help elect Barack Obama at $1,400-$2,200 a month.

"They don't need that," she said, pointing at the salary figures. "People should volunteer, they shouldn't get paid. You're doing a bad thing." She, of course, didn't give me time to respond, but I didn't give her much satisfaction. I assumed a quizzical expression and told her I didn't understand. It was my strategy with people who wanted to give me attitude, one I used for the remainder of my time canvassing. I figured out then that people get no happiness from trying to be snippy with someone who doesn't appear to understand. Some of them would come back to apologize, but would go away thinking they got the last word. This particular woman was so frustrated she had to remind me again what she thought of me. She passed by my table again with some colleagues, and I wasn't going to say anything. But she pointed at me.

"I already told you what I think about you," she said. I just threw up my hands to show her I wasn't going to pay her any mind, and went back to recruiting. She wasn't going to throw me out of my mood. She wasn't going to have that power. I was a white guy trying to help elect a black president on the campus of the oldest historically black college in the nation. I was standing right down the street from where Josh Gibson used to smash the longest home runs anyone's ever seen, and nothing was going to stop me from having a great day.

Besides, it's not just that this woman was rude. She was wrong in her assumption that people who got involved were rubbing their hands together, scheming on ways to spend the fortune they would exploit from this election. I could have told her about Adelsia, who canvassed for us during the day and worked the red-eye shift at CVS at night so she could support her children. Adelsia talked about her love for Janis Joplin during Question of the Day in the mornings, and, when I told her I admired her dedication for the way she worked two jobs, she just shrugged.

"A lot of people do it," she said. "I've got to do this to support my family, so it's just got to be done. It's nothing special."

I could have mentioned Jessica, a middle-aged former elementary teacher. She worked for us for about a month before she decided, like most people, that canvassing wasn't for her. She was a successful canvasser, but the truth is that most people want to give to young, energetic kids, and most older people can't handle the physical toll of canvassing. It's very difficult for individuals who have held jobs with more legitimate outfits to stay on in one with so few normal aspects of employment. So she quit and came back two weeks later for her paycheck. I'll never forget the dejected look when I handed her that check. It was two weeks' worth of minimum wage.

"This isn't even enough to make rent," she said. She had to sit down, and I could tell she was rifling through her brain for some way to be able to pay. She looked like she had been punched. I hated Progressive Futures for telling a loving person like Jessica who wanted to get involved in this election that she could do so and make a living. It's disgusting that people are led to believe that canvassing can be a ticket to solvency when, in all likelihood, it will exacerbate their problems. People like Jessica came to us because they wanted to help give more Americans access to a living wage, but they didn't get paid one while they were with us.

If you've ever looked in the eyes of an individual who makes minimum wage, you know that it's not enough. This myth that anyone who works hard in this country will succeed is as insulting as it is false. Adelsia had to work 18 hours a day to give her family the basic necessities, and working for CVS is a dead end job. How is she going to advance her career when she has to sleep at some point? Jessica's case makes me just as livid. Here we have a national shortage of teachers, and this woman, with the kind of love in her heart that would make boys and girls grow up to be adults with love in their hearts, can't keep doing what she loved for a living. She came to PFI because she wants to change things in this country, and all I can do is hand her a damn minimum wage check.

I think a lot about Adelsia and Jessica, but I also think a lot about Chris Crump. He was a middle-aged black guy who came in for a couple of days but didn't make staff. Not being familiar with the area, I sent Chris to canvass in Crystal City, an area of Arlington where the Boeing office sits right next to the Lockheed Martin office and the Kellog Brown Root offices. Nobody in his group did well, but Chris had a rough time of it. He said he felt like a black man begging for money in the South. He didn't come back after that day, but I saw him when he came in for his check.

"Hey man, do you know about any jobs?"

I shook my head. "Only canvassing jobs."

He nodded. "That's what I figured." I don't know Chris Crump, but I have a picture of him in my mind. He's at home sitting with his bare feet resting on an old coffee table. He's wearing an undershirt and a pair of old jeans, and he's drinking a beer, wondering how in the hell he's going to make ends meet and why in the hell he burned two days trying to canvass with a bunch of crazy young people.

I know there are factory owners who once lived in their cars. I know there are children of deadbeat dads who went on to become president. I know some people feel they can do anything they set their minds to and want to hold on to their hard-earned money instead of giving it to bureaucrats. I just don't understand the many people who can think only of themselves. We are one of the wealthiest nations in the world, and we can't even ensure that a strong, smart woman like Adelsia can spend her nights and weekends at home raising her kids instead of selling sodas to sorority girls. Working in the service industry isn't a ticket out of poverty, it's a ticket into it. Dubya and his buddies would know that if they ever tried living on 7 bucks an hour or stopped to consider someone who has.

These are the real economic matters that candidates should debate, but they never do. Poverty was not an issue in the 2008 election, and it didn't come up in the first presidential debate on September 26th. For a time, some wondered whether there would be a debate at all. The economic meltdown had motivated McCain to consider "suspending" his campaign until the bank bailout bill passed. This was a dumb decision. I didn't need hallucinogenic drugs to know it at the time, though. In the first place, the public wouldn't buy into the idea that a politician could stop campaigning in an election year, especially one who was running for president. In the second place, the bank bailout was not the kind of bill that would make people love its champion, even if John McCain could in any way, shape, or form claim that a bill straight from Hank Paulson and Ben Bernanke was his. What did he conceive of saying to the crowds in rural Pennsylvania? "Because of my efforts, we gave $700 billion in taxpayer money to wealthy bankers!" I have my doubts that this would have been a real applause line anywhere, let alone for the hate-filled zealots who would begin to fill his rallies in the coming weeks.

Obama made exactly the right move, which was no move. PBS wasn't calling off the debate, and he reiterated that he would be there. Americans don't allow presidential candidates to run for office at their convenience, so McCain was there, too.

Everyone went out to a bar called The Big Hunt to watch it. We were becoming quite a group. There were a lot of us recent college grads doing this to make ends meet while we elected Barack Obama and all the Democrats. There was Ryan, who people called "Quiet Ryan" in college but was always the first guy to the bar. There was Lindsay, who played rugby and talked in a very blunt manner whenever she felt strange about something, which was often. There was Zach, the best canvasser on staff because he asked people if they were Democrats, then launched into the rap without asking if they had a minute. There were others, many others, and they shared my interests and believed in me as I believed in them. We developed the camaraderie that all people develop when they share experiences.

And, without knowing it, I had initiated many shared experiences with Albertine. She was one of the best canvassers immediately, and, when I realized that one of my biggest responsibilities for the office was drawing up the canvassing crews for the day, I saw to it that I found out why every day. She had a disarming smile that made people want to tell her everything and made donors want to give her all the money they had. In the course of riding the Metro with her to and from Chinatown, or walking down to M and 19th, or K and 15th, I began to enjoy her company. We spoke of office-related topics mostly, but there was an edge of humor or sass to our conversations which, to me, suggested she enjoyed my company, nothing more. I didn't think I was anything in her mind because a woman with freckles apportioned perfectly all over her face and bright brown eyes who wore interesting hanging earrings to go with her complicated pony-tail had to have some kind of an arrangement with a guy. I didn't want to ask, though. I refused to ask, because I didn't want to hear a name of some kind and visualize him with the gorgeous woman who was not obtainable to me.

And yet, at this time, when I was sure that I could not have been anything in her eyes, she told me later that she was trying to devise a way for us to interact in a non-work setting. She said that she thought I'd enjoy coming over to her apartment to swim. Had I known this, I would have jumped out of my clothes and into my swim trunks and run down the highway to her apartment at the first chance. No thought would have given me more pleasure, and no action would have felt better at the time. And yet no knowledge would have kept future good times from happening with such certainty. The fact that I did not know, and wouldn't have suspected, made me look infinitely better in her eyes. She perceived my deference as indifference. How or why this could be the case is a mystery of love, but the fact that my thoughts did not match her perception of them did not augur well.

But I went to the Big Hunt on the night of the first debate with no knowledge or expectation of any of this. I went there because I wanted to get drunk and watch the debate with friends. All of us had quite a laugh when Obama began the debate by saying, "At this defining moment in our nation," which was the opening line of our rap. Then it was on. I started throwing down Pabst Blue Ribbons and passing them out to everyone I could. I hadn't gotten drunk in weeks, and it was time to celebrate. I hardly paid attention to the debate once I realized that neither candidate would make any gaffes and more important matters appeared.

Albertine was more interesting to me than the debate. It was one of those times when inebriated persons are pushed together by the effects of drink, and, before one or the other realizes what is happening, there is a very public display of affection.

I could not believe it was happening. I had assumed that a woman like her would already be attached to someone, and I had not reserved any hope that we might come together. But I knew something was coming from these women who had shunned me for so long. I was constantly around intelligent women who wanted to talk politics, wanted to talk about the problems in the world, and didn't think I was boring or weird. I noticed that the women I met through the office or through friends had begun to listen to me in the mode of a captive audience that is so integral to canvassing, and I could tell they wanted to hear what I had to say.

One time on the GW campus, I was standing under an umbrella in the pouring rain when a beautiful co-ed came up. She had forgotten her umbrella and had been running to get out of the rain, and she panted to catch her breath. I said the rap without thinking about it and didn't care that she didn't want to give money. We locked eyes and she was smiling at me with that look that women give to an interesting stranger, and I wanted to throw the umbrella away and run through the rain with her. I couldn't believe that, if only for a moment, a woman like this could feel attracted to me.

I still hadn't had any more success since I moved to DC, mostly because I didn't have time. There were many women whom I wanted to ask out, but I couldn't ask them to meet me at 10:30 on Wednesday night when I had just worked fourteen hours and needed to do so again the next day. It was frustrating, but also comforting because someone who works those hours has no time to feel deprived of love.

I learned something that night. I had made no moves toward Albertine. I had enjoyed her company, but I didn't make any stammering requests to get coffee some time. She initiated that night's activities, but I was only there to accept her advances because I hadn't tripped over myself making advances of my own. It occurred to me that this had been my mistake in so many previous attempts with women. That was the first thing Albertine taught me.

Chapter 16

From Poem in October

O may my heat's truth
Still be sung
On this high hill in a year's turning.
-Dylan Thomas

I won my third and last $500 contribution on a cold and rainy afternoon. I was in the Woodley Park neighborhood, just down Connecticut Avenue from the National Zoo, and I was standing a few steps from the tall escalator I had ascended three and a half months earlier arriving in D.C. It was astounding how much I had changed from that day, from a bewildered college graduate trying to find his way to a determined fundraiser with no impulse to come in out of the rain.

I had success right away that day. A guy parked his convertible outside CVS to go inside for a quick purchase. When he came out, he told me he had already given to the DNC. I launched right into the "Iowa story" that Dan had taught everyone to give to repeat contributors, saying, "I really appreciate what you've done for us this year. That's the kind of involvement we need to win this historic election. But I would also like to remind you of Iowa during the 2004 election. John Kerry lost Iowa by less than 10,000 votes. If the DNC had just one more field office in Iowa, we could have made over 43,000 more voter contacts in that state and, in all likelihood, turned it our way. Now, one field office costs only $5,000, but you can see the level of impact that one of these offices can have. In that spirit, I would ask if you would be willing to maximize your personal impact on this election, and give again."

The guy had been stepping into his car, but what I said stopped him in his tracks.

"You're doing a great job," he told me. "Can you hold on a minute? I think I have a check in my car." He did, and he made a $250 contribution. It was one of those times that makes canvassing so rewarding, when you can make a stranger believe in you enough to donate a significant amount of money on a whim. It put a smile on my face.

That smile was still there when the jolly portly fellow who owned a nearby Indian restaurant came outside to greet me.

"Are you guys here again? You come everyday and I don't know why."

I tried to explain why, but he cut me off with a wave of the hand.

"No, no that's not important. You are young and handsome, and I'm old and ugly, and I'm telling you that you shouldn't be out here. Let me ask you, are you paid well?"

I told him the truth, and he shook his head.

"You are like homeless person, standing outside and begging for money. You young people are capable, and this is all they allow you to do." I thanked him for his compliments, but he didn't know how much I loved what I was doing.

Later in the day, a black man in an Ole Miss hat approached me and asked if I knew why it was ironic that he was wearing an Ole Miss hat. Not wanting to speak candidly about race in my blue DNC shirt, I told him I didn't know. He asked if I had ever heard of segregation. I couldn't wait any longer and I said of course I had, and I knew the story of James Meredith desegregating that campus in 1962, and the struggle of blacks to gain access to higher education in the South. He nodded his head and told me he liked what I was doing. When he asked if I had any spare change, I gave him all the change I had in my pocket. Out of all the times I was asked for spare change while I was canvassing, that was the only time I gave it. In a sense, he had canvassed me.

It was the other way around most of the day. A beautiful middle-aged woman stopped and told me how she had been a Hillary supporter, but had recently made a donation to the Obama campaign after the emergence of Palin. That left an opening for me to make my argument concerning the best way to supplement her generous gift to the Obama campaign. She thought for a moment, and agreed, but the rain had started to come down, so I suggested we step under a nearby overhang. I remember the way she skipped to that overhang as if I were a lover she was leading to a tryst. She declined to match her generous gift to the Obama campaign, but she made out a $500 check. And I never got ill will from a former Hillary supporter again after the 2008 Republican National Convention.

The $500 put my total for that day at $836, my best day ever. I didn't know it at the time, but I would never again crack $400 on a day. As October wore on, the election was no longer in doubt to people in D.C. Obama had regained control of the race, building a six to ten point lead in most polls, and Sarah Palin began to make a fool of herself on a daily basis. On top of that, people began to grow tired of being solicited, and it was easy to understand their frustration. Most donors had given more money in this election than they ever had before, and they couldn't fathom why we were still asking for it, given Obama's vast financial advantage over McCain. It was a sentiment best summed up by a woman near Metro Center who said to me, "Hey buddy, why don't you pipe down?" And though I could understand her irritation, three solid months of canvassing had made it impossible to get the last word with me in the street.

"I can't pipe down, ma'am," I said. "I'm too excited about this election!" She knew she wouldn't get anywhere with me and kept walking.

Perhaps she could also tell I was speaking the truth. I felt let loose in those days. Never in my life had I shared as much with people that side of my personality that is the grinning ridiculousness of my frequent use of hyperbolic gesticulations. Given a position of leadership, I felt free to say what came in to my mind in a way that I never had before and never have since.

The most liberating aspect of it was the way I was received by those around me. I saw they could feel the passion I had for this election and I did anything I could to make them laugh. And they did, often, and I loved them for it. I told them how my middle school football coach had given me a lesson apropos to canvassing when he said, "I don't care if you're shoveling shit. You take pride in what you do and do it right. Toby, go get me a large diet Coke." I told them how one of my basketball coaches had played me at point guard even though I didn't like it because he was an anti-Semite, and how one game, when I was turning the ball over again and again, I heard my dad shout from the stands, "Toby, our team's in white!" I feel so often when I tell stories like this that people don't understand that I say these things to bring a smile to their face, not to invite pity. In the past, these sorts of self-deprecating stories would elicit looks of sympathy in people for a person who was still so depressed about meaningless childhood sports exploits to share these stories. In that tiny office in Dupont above Zorba's Greek Café, my colleagues gave me the esteem necessary to have fun at my expense without worrying about hurt feelings that weren't there. When they laughed at my anecdotes and voices and personality, they gave me a strength and confidence I never knew I had. It was the first time in my life that I felt understood.

Albertine had a lot to do with it. For years, women had been one of the biggest chips on my shoulder. I had never felt deprived of love, only a certain type of it. I knew filial love from the support of a loving family and an appreciation for those gifts I have that can only be inherited. I knew fraternal love from friends who have taught me so much about life and shared treasured experiences with me. I knew the love of the world that comes from the written word, music, and all forms of art, and I knew the reverence of nature.

But I also knew a hundred secret paths I wanted to walk down with a lover, a thousand thoughts that I wanted to share with a lover, a million tiny displays of affection I wanted to give to a lover. I perceived that I lacked the satisfaction of sex, but it wasn't my focus. I yearned for the type of companionship that can only come from love, and I was jealous of the people who had it. I saw the guys I got looked over for time and time again, and I judged them using the strict criteria I use with myself. These boyfriends had no appreciation for the improving qualities of all women or the one who privileged them with their company. They spoke in commonplace trivialities and resisted knowledge of the arts. I would have done anything to replace them in their lover's arms, and this wish only made matters worse, I knew, because my desperation never failed to overshadow the qualities that make me attractive. The kind of love I yearned to share, with no external outlet, used to come back as a dagger of self-loathing and self-pity, hatred for innocent people, and disdain for women. I used to have these thoughts at night.

Albertine extinguished these thoughts when she brought me into her life. The first exchange we had, initiated by the heightened sense that comes from tequila, gave way to others that may have been sober but not sobering. When I took days off for Rosh Hoshanah and Yom Kippur, we spent those days together and found what other times we could in those busy days. I'll never again feel myself inadequate, and I'll never again hate people for having something I've never had.

Those prior yearnings may have left me, but they were replaced by a yearning to see Albertine every hour of the day. I became impatient to get the day over with at the office so I could call her. I became bored at social gatherings because I wanted to speak only to her. I called none of my friends because I no longer thought of them. My desire to be with her was unquenchable. It didn't cease when we had spent a night together; it only increased when I dropped her off at her apartment.

In the same way, the aspects of our relationship that were affirming did not clarify the many puzzling components of it. She was a spiritual person. Nobody can carry around a face and frame like hers without feeling some connection with the powers that determine the thousand coincidences of each millisecond. Albertine came into contact with them each week at yoga, and read about them in the Buddhist-themed books that her instructors recommended. On several occasions, she spoke to me about the need to eliminate the ego. And she said it with the same musical expressiveness that her voice always had.

Yet, I couldn't help noticing occasions when Buddhist teachings would have counseled in direct contradiction to the actions she took or the thoughts she professed. This was truest when she would take the opportunity to remind me that I was not her boyfriend. In so doing, she was showing an attachment to terminology, particularly the misguided notions others might have about terminology, a factor that was entirely out of her or my control. When she would tell me again to make sure I knew that I wasn't her boyfriend, I would become quiet until she could see that I didn't care how she referred to us and I didn't care how others referred to us. I only wanted there to be an us.

But her voice and mannerisms were something special. She had a short way of speaking sometimes when I made her laugh or said something she liked. "You're funny," she would say, or "You're a dork," or "You're cute," or "You're sweet." The phrases contained the kind of affection that only lovers are privy to. They filled me with elation. I saw in them the simplicity of one word sentences from Whitman, and all the pureness of feelings evoked by Whitman's words came to me whenever I felt them wash over my ears.

On the other hand, I sensed some degree to which she felt I was too strange. I remember a time when I replied to her "You're a dork' by calling her a dork, and she stiffly denied it. I thought she had misunderstood me, and asked her again if she didn't think she was some kind of a dork because I thought anybody who spent time with one wouldn't mind submitting to being called one. She disagreed again with a serious look, so I dropped it.

It was because of that episode that I refused to share with her the thoughts in the poetry of William Carlos Williams. I was reading his selected poems, and the volume lay on the desk next to my bed at Stan and Jenny's. One night, in that wonderful naked aftermath, she picked it up and began leafing through it.

"How's this?" It was a question I had been waiting years to hear, on the many occasions when I read a poem and wished that another person were there to experience the particular ecstasy of a poet. The image of a lover in my arms reading the same words with me and sharing them had been inscribed in my mind. Yet, at that moment, something else in my head told me to wait and see if she turned to a particular page and started reading.

"It's amazing. He really likes trees." This glib assessment of one of the giants of poetry would have been rejected out of hand by anyone who loved poetry or knew that I would never be this simplistic in my love for anything. But it seemed to satisfy Albertine. She put the volume back on the desk.

"I really like trees, too." Whenever I remember this moment, I see that the course of our relationship was meant to be the way it turned out. The feelings induced by works of art must be shared with others, particularly the person you love. I was in love with Albertine, it's true, but these feelings, without their proper recipient, can produce the acts which at the time seem foolish because they have quickened a lover's departure. In reality, they are a reflection of the connection that must occur in any longstanding love.

I was not unhappy on the night of the William Carlos Williams incident, though. How could I have been unhappy? I was discovering the parts of a woman's company that I had known I would value, but that I had never experienced before. I'm not referring only to the physical pleasures. I'm referring to easing into Sunday with a nice breakfast. I'm referring to the times she used the mirror on the rattan table to arrange herself and I couldn't help but grin at my reflection. And I'm referring to the time she met Eddie and talked his ear off as if making an effort to impress him. There were times when my giddiness seemed an attractive quality to her. On those occasions, she returned my smile with her own. She said frequently that my enthusiasm made her feel like she was rediscovering the joys of companionship.

On several other occasions, she would chafe at being connected with a person who had never had another lover. She often said I expected too much of her time and thoughts because I didn't know what it was like to be in a relationship. When she said this, she inflicted pain on me because she brought up the loneliness that came before her in my life. It was as if the fact that no woman saw what she saw in me before her were my choice and my fault, and there was nothing I could say to counter her argument. But these times were rare, and indeed, late in our relationship. Initially, they were far off, and my times with Albertine were ones of great happiness.

I managed not to enjoy every moment of the happiest month of my life. My hunger to be with Albertine was only one example. I was too caught up to understand that everything would be over in a month and I would never be able to go back. Instead of savoring every minute as I would now if I got the chance, I complained to myself. I seethed at Ellen for not answering the phone in the morning while I was trying to assign our canvassers. I threw a chair across the room in a rage that the payroll office had sent me the wrong spreadsheet. I whined about my checking account when I had to front the money for pizza. It's the mundane aspects of life that keep us from enjoying the best times of our lives. It's a curse we can't know until the times we cherish are over. I never would have believed it if someone told me the speed with which this magical time would come to a close, but I wish someone had tried. I also wish that, at some point, I'll again be as happy as I was in October 2008.

The tedium of some of my duties could infuriate me, but there were people, who, perhaps unknowingly, made my tasks enjoyable. I hated doing the daily deposit to the national office in

Boston. It involved the aggregation and confirmation of every dollar we had raised the day before, as well as multiple errands. I often referred to it as "the daily ordeal." The first trip was to pick up money orders, since you don't send cash in the mail. For these, we had gone to a CVS just down the street from the office for these, but a change in management made things difficult. The new manager would not make money orders totaling more than $1,000. I argued with him, telling him he was obstructing Barack Obama's path to the White House, but he wouldn't budge. Luckily, I found a liquor store on L and 19th named Barmy Liquors where a guy named Mickey whipped up money orders in five minutes with no problems at all. Mickey and his shopkeepers were Jordanians, and they had quite a scene in their store. They bantered to each other and flirted with every woman who walked in the store. No woman was "ma'am" there. She was "darling" or "sweetheart," regardless of looks or age. One time a toothless, homeless woman was leaving the store when she turned around and said to the swarthy bald guy who always wore striped dress shirts with the top two buttons undone, "I'll be back for your clothes." He looked up from his register and said, "Thank you, Mama!" It wasn't just this kind of color that made me like going to Barmy's. Once, Mickey and I were talking about a debate the night before.

"McCain is so worried about people who make over $250,000 a year," Mickey told me. "I don't understand. They're not the ones we should be worried about. We don't need to worry about people who have jobs, a house, two cars, and health insurance. We should be worried about people who have none of those things." I think it was this wisdom of Mickey the liquor store owner which won out over Joe the plumber; it also won out over decades of the rich convincing working people to vote against their pocketbooks.

The next step was a trip to Fedex Kinkos, and I preferred the one down 20th Street from the office. I liked that particular one because of a woman named Anne there who called me rubber band man because I always asked for any extra rubber bands she had. She and the other employees there were always having a laugh about something. They made fun of each other, played jokes, and talked about last weekend in a way that made me want to join in. Anne asked me every day how I was doing, and I would always say, "I'm hanging in there." And she would smile and say, "Hey, that's all we can do." One time, she was walking with a friend when I was canvassing, and she pushed her friend into making a contribution. I gave her one of my Obama buttons.

With the daily deposit finished, it was usually time to go to Zorba's for a bite to eat. I tried not to go there too much, because a mere gyro platter would put my budget at risk. But then Saul started giving me discounts. He saw me going in and out of the office all the time, and we got to talking.

"I see you guys up there every night, working your asses off," he said. "I feel you're doing it for all of us, for working people."

It was the perfect verbalization of a thought I'd had for so long, that if working people in this country could just stick together, there's so much that could be changed. If everyone thought of each other as neighbors and not competitors, if everyone behind a counter or a desk wanted to be as helpful as possible to his fellow man and not take glee in exerting power, if everyone could take responsibility instead of blaming it on the guy one step up or down the totem poll, I guarantee you everyone would have health care and higher education. And if working people in this country ever gain the understanding that there are more working people than wealthy people, they'll be the bosses. If the election of Barack Obama is the first step toward a politicization of working people, the possibilities are limitless. Even if that never happens, though, Anne and Saul and Mickey will be friends of mine.

Saul hit it right on the head that day in a way that none of the candidates did. All the debates were discouraging, the vice presidential one most of all. In these days, I was working fourteen hours a day because I thought this election was about health care for all Americans and an end to the war in Iraq, and all Joe Biden was able to do was get the message across that he was from Scranton and therefore had just as much small-town credibility as Sarah Palin. The veep nominees traded "Say it ain't so, Joe," and "My father always taught me to get back up." It was a contest to see who could claim to be more homespun, an insult to every voter's intelligence and a despicable display of the personality-centered politics we have cultivated in this country. The better candidate is not necessarily the one who has the more compelling personal story. The better candidate is the smarter one, the one who will work harder, and the one who cares the most about fixing the country's problems. I didn't think either of them were the better candidate that night.

Then there were the networks, compiling up-to-the-millisecond polling of undecided voters. People who have not decided their vote less than a month before the election are the sort of fools who vote on a whim. The networks are wrong to think that there's value to be found in the momentary impulses of such goobers. It's supposed to be a discussion of the issues, not a boxing match. The debates are there to make each candidate defend their positions and challenge one another, not to have Anderson Cooper sitting in a room with twelve random people from Ohio who believe his or her undecided status has somehow turned them into experts. It was frustrating to work my ass off in anticipation of these debates only to see them turn into the continuation of horse-race election coverage.

One thing of value about the debates was that they always gave us a chance to get drunk together after a hard day's work. On every debate night, I tuned out the meaningless drivel from the television and tuned into my co-workers. And we had a blast.

Reggie, the Vietnam veteran, was one of our leaders. It was easy to see the love he had for us. He greeted everyone who walked in with glee, he talked to everyone and let them know why he thought they were great people, and he drank more than anyone else. The vice presidential debate was the first time I realized that he was an alcoholic. He took me aside at one point and told me I was coming with him on Friday.

"On Friday night, Toby, you coming with me," he said, poking me in the shoulder. "I'll pick you up from the office, and you'll come back to my house for dinner. Then we're gonna hit up the town, we're gonna go dancing and do it up right."

I laughed and told him I had to work late on Friday like every other day. The smile disappeared from his face.

"Freeze!" he said. "Eyes on me! You're coming with me on Friday and I won't talk any more about it." I laughed again, but I excused myself to get away. These phrases were what made him such an endearing person, but when he got drunk, they became ominous. It was more unsettling later when he had me drive his Cadillac to Stan and Jenny's from where we were watching the debate. It was a short drive, but I hadn't planned on driving, and I shouldn't have been behind the wheel after drinking. It was better than having Reggie drive, though. He was falling asleep in the passenger seat. When I got to Stan and Jenny's, he groaned and got out of the car.

"Let me have my keys," he said. Upon getting them back from me, he climbed behind the wheel and began muttering. "He's gonna take himself home. Just himself. How you going to just drive yourself home?" I tried to reason with him, but he was rolling out of the driveway before I knew it. He did make it home that night, and he was at the office the next day. But I learned more about dying of cancer at that moment than I ever have before.

Chapter 17

The Dance

> In Brueghel's great picture, The Kermess,
> the dancers go round, they go round and
> around, the squel and the blare and the
> tweedle of bag pipes, a bugle and fiddles
> tipping their bellies (round as the thick-
> sided glasses whose wash they impound)
> their hips and their bellies off balance
> to turn them. Kicking and rolling about
> the Fair Grounds, swinging their butts, those
> shanks must be sound to bear up under such
> rollicking measures, prance as they dance
> in Brueghel's great picture, The Kermess
>
> -William Carlos Williams

I was packing my envelope at FedEx Kinkos in Dupont when a shiny-headed man ambled up to the door and pushed in when he should have pulled. The length of time that elapsed during his pushing amazed me. When he got the door open, he came in and looked around, unsure of his surroundings.

"How can I make a shipment?" he asked Anne. She pointed out the envelopes and shipment forms.

"How do I make copies?" he replied. Anne motioned to the copy machine right next to the envelopes.

"And where is the fax machine?" he said. Anne showed him the fax machine on a table next to the copier. When it occurred to him that the entire dialogue could have been avoided by a better sense of observation, he frowned and walked over to the copier next to me. With empathy for a guy negotiating the complexities of a copy joint for the first time, I showed him how to work the copier. I noticed "Republican National Committee" on some of the papers he was copying.

"I believe I work for the other team," I said. "I'm shipping out DNC contributions." He laughed.

"That's funny. I'm sending out contributions, too." I couldn't resist a joke.

"Are you sending them to Michigan?" He was good-natured enough to laugh at my allusion to the recent news that McCain had pulled out of Michigan. The state had been the focus of attention because there was an understanding that, without Michigan, the electoral mathematics would not be there for a McCain victory. The news about Michigan sealed Obama's victory in my mind. I knew that an election can shift overnight, but I thought Obama was going to win.

That's why I brought up Michigan, but I also did so because it seemed that the man, whose gleaming scalp reminded me of Adam Schmidt, the former Bush strategist who was running McCain's campaign, was dumber than me and worked less hard. I was in my natural habitat of packing off money to Boston, and he was invading my territory. I'd never once thought of Republicans as fellow participants in a great American democratic experiment. They were the other side, and I wanted my side to win.

The office was a joyous place to be. The phone had begun to ring less, and I got to enjoy the company of the other directors. We spent the day engaged in our duties but conversing on the encouraging progress of the election. I kept everyone up to date on the Iowa Electronics Market, which allows investors to buy $1 dollar shares of either McCain or Obama winning the election. These "winshares" were far in Obama's favor. Fivethirtyeight.com, a site Dan knew, proved to be a treasure trove of data. I enjoyed analyzing the continuous graphs, but I also enjoyed the descriptions of the respective field offices in swing state communities. The Obama offices were full of energetic people of all ages ready to go door-to-door or make calls and the McCain offices had high-tech phone stations that were empty, with a few old people coming by to pick up yard signs. Even that boring old curmudgeon David Broder, who, like most columnists, uses words like "rightly" far too much, noticed that the Democratic ground game was far superior.

There was a collective pride in the office for that ground game. We saw ourselves as critical to its execution and success, and we were sure it would succeed. We would laugh our asses off while we counted the money we raised.

I believe people like us were the reason Obama won. There was a mythical story about a canvasser visiting a rural house in a swing state. The story varied as to whether it took place in central Pennsylvania or Indiana or the "real" Virginia, as McCain's state director referred to it, but it always went the same way. The canvasser knocked on the door, and a woman answered. The canvasser asked her if she would mind sharing who she was voting for in the election.

The woman answers, "I'm not sure." She calls back to her husband, who's watching some game, asking, "Honey, who are we voting for this year?"

"Tell 'em not to worry," the guy says. "We're votin' for the nigger." This story spread because it contained a kernel of truth. There were door-to-door volunteers visiting their neighbors to tell them to vote for a black man in some of the most racist parts of America. Rep. John Murtha professes the same love for Pennsylvania that every politician professes for his home district, but he called his home state racist. And yet there were thousands, if not millions, of people who had the audacity to go to strangers' houses on behalf of Barack Obama. There were many other anecdotes out there about canvassers being threatened with violence, and a few with real violence, but the field organizers, volunteers, and canvassers cared enough about the course of politics to keep knocking. They doubtless overcame many fears to do so, just as millions of people who voted for Obama overcame prejudices to do so.

I said this to keep people motivated, but I still believe it: It was the canvasser, the team leader, the organizer who would win this election and ultimately did. As much as we joked around the office about Howard Dean being our "godfather" or our "fearless leader," we knew he wasn't the one who would win the election. The strategies he initiated may have formed the skeleton of the operation, but we were its body.

I did my best to keep our people in positive spirits toward the end. Canvassing was becoming more difficult, as astute Washingtonians knew Obama had the election. People began to use the excuse of the economy the way people who have the least to worry about verbalize their worries the most. It doesn't have basis in fact, but this excuse does reveal that a person is no longer interested in making a donation. I didn't care. I didn't want canvassers who had labored on this election to have a sour taste in their mouths at the end. So I told them it was us who was winning this election. And I told them we had a chance to disprove Tupac Shakur's prediction that "We ain't ready to see a black President" and LBJ's prediction that the South was lost to the Democrats forever. And I made a connection between the way working people were throwing themselves behind Obama to the way working people in the South and Midwest came together as Populists about a hundred years ago. And I compared the last days of this election to the sweetest part of a cup of coffee with sugar in it, the last few drops. It was an analogy I felt secure in making because I now drank coffee every morning before work, scheming what I could say to people and hoping they would laugh and believe it.

Dan gave everyone a new strategy to squeeze all the money we could from the streets: the Saxby strategy. Nobody was worried about the presidential race, so we needed to remind people of the possibility of a filibuster-proof majority in the Senate. The best example of a Republican who would need to go down on November 4th was Saxby Chambliss of Georgia. In the last two weeks, Dan and I referred to canvassers who raised more than $400 in a day as Georgia peaches and we adopted a lewd pop song called "Peaches 'n' Cream" as our office theme song.

People I was canvassing would say, "Well, I've already given, so I think I'm tapped out for this year."

"I definitely understand," I would reply. "I really appreciate all the support you've given us this year. Have you heard of Saxby Chambliss?" Many would think for a second and plead ignorance.

"Well, you might remember him from the 2002 senatorial election in Georgia, where Chambliss beat the Democratic incumbent Max Cleland by portraying him as unpatriotic. Cleland was a triple-amputee Vietnam veteran, and Chambliss put a picture of him between Saddam Hussein and Osama Bin Laden in a campaign commercial. That worked in 2002, but Chambliss is up for re-election this year against a Decmocrat named Jim Martin, who is underfunded and understaffed but only one to two percentage points away from defeating Saxby Chambliss. Now if Martin should win, in all likelihood, we'll have the 60 seats in the Senate we need for a filibuster-proof majority. In that spirit, I'll ask you if you could maximize your impact on this historic election and make one more donation this year."

The astute donor would have agreed with me, then gone back to the office to make a last minute donation to the Democratic Senatorial Campaign Committee or to Jim Martin's campaign, but nobody did. Many people who had already given felt compelled to give.

"I wasn't going to give again," one woman told me. "But then you brought up Saxby Chambliss." She gave $200.

We kept canvassing up to the end, as Dan indicated that our office would keep raising money through the Friday before the election. My last day canvassing was the Thursday before the election, when I went back to the George Washington bust on the GW campus in Foggy Bottom. I raised $239 that day and encountered no ill-wishers. I had learned to smile in a way that would make almost everyone passed smile back, and it was a gorgeous day. My favorite donor that day was a young woman who worked at the checkout counter of the GW Hospital food court. I got her to give $72 because John McCain is 72 years old. It was my pleasure to thank her by giving her one of those artsy "Change" Obama posters that were everywhere then; someone had handed it to me earlier in the day. I hope she put it up on her wall at home and pays attention to Obama's fate in office and politics for the rest of her life.

The $239 I raised that day pushed my total personal amount of money raised over $17,000. I think there were three more field offices because of the money I raised, or one more commercial on the air in an obscure race somewhere, or hundreds of bus tickets from D.C. to Crawford, Texas.

Everyone in the office knew his or her totals. Dan added up our total personal amounts, and the numbers were gratifying for everyone. He also had us keeping close watch on our total amount raised as an office for the fall. He had set a goal of $471,000, which would be $1,000 for every national race a Democrat was participating in, but that figure was far off. Then he brought out $300,000, which we were able to reach the second-to-last week. Of course, then he raised it to $320,000, and when we got that, to $350,00. I never did understand the goal-setting of PFI and why it had so many proponents. It's not because I can't comprehend the concept that a person will keep that figure in mind and use it as motivation. What I don't understand is the idea that people can be motivated at so many different times by so many different numbers. And in canvassing, where there is no end until the end of the campaign, these benchmarks that fluctuate cannot be seen as goals by anyone who knows that there won't be any rewards, financial or otherwise, to come from meeting the goals. All there will be is a new goal.

The goals that Dan put out were not the only reason I began to trust him less at the end of the election. He became vague whenever I asked him about the plans of the national office. I know headquarters kept many people in the dark, but Dan never could be clear about the last few days before the election. At the start of the fall, we had been told about a wild 96-hour get out the vote operation that we would be running in the last few days, but, as we got closer to those last hours, nobody knew anything about it. I was attracted to the idea, as many in the office were, because we liked the idea of bringing the election home by working our asses off in the final hours. I asked Dan about it all the time and he said it would happen, but he never had any details.

On the Tuesday before Election Day, Dan called me at 10 p.m. to tell me to get on a conference call for our region. He said I would find out about what we'd be doing the last few days before the election. The call was thirty minutes of regional director Adam Jacobs talking, and I didn't care for what he had to say. Our office would be switching to a fundraising office for Save the Children, and we were to prepare everyone for it by trying to convince them to stay on staff as Save the Children canvassers after the election. There were no plans for a get-out-the-vote, but Adam did set a goal of $500,000 for the region by the end of the week, and talked a lot about the idea of "marathon" canvassing days where door canvassers could street canvass during the day then go door-to-door at night. When one of the other directors who did payroll for his office asked how we would go about giving people overtime for canvassing for thirteen hours in a day, Adam said we shouldn't promise them overtime.

The next morning I told Dan that Friday would be my last day. I had no interest in working for Save the Children. He complained that three day's notice was hardly enough time. I just looked at him blankly, not even entertaining the thought that normal labor practices applied for an organization that paid me about half of minimum wage.

There was a lot to enjoy about these last days, though. I had new friends and I had Albertine. I knew I was quitting PFI, but I also knew then that I wanted to stay in D.C. for good, and she was a big part of that decision. She was the first woman to believe in me enough to give me the time of day.

Eddie thought that was a bullshit reason to stay in D.C. He told me so over beers one night. A couple of days earlier, he had left a drunk voicemail for me on my phone in which he revealed his disappointment that we had not made time to enjoy each other's company recently.

"What the fuck is this? It's Saturday night, man, and you don't answer my call or return it later in the night? That's completely gay, man. You heard me. I said gay. I know you don't like it when I say things are gay when things are gay, but you're acting completely gay right now." The message itself was less endearing than Eddie's typical vehemence. I didn't get in touch with him that night because I was with Albertine, but I was happy to arrange for beers the following week.

"All I'm saying, man, is you should never move to a city over a girl," he said. "That shouldn't be the only factor."

"It's not," I said. "I love it here. I've made a bunch of friends and I like the Metro. I should just stay here and see how this thing turns out with her. I don't know if you know, but I've wanted to be with someone for awhile."

"Oh, I'm well aware of that."

"Well, this is my chance. So I'm going to do it. If it doesn't work, D.C. is as good a place as any to live."

"Fair enough. She is reasonably hot, I'd say. And she definitely seemed like your type when I met her."

I laughed. "My type. What do you mean?"

"Oh, you know. Good-looking but a personality that makes her appear better looking and concerned about the world. 'What do you want to do?' she kept asking me. She was getting a little intense about that. I was like 'Hey, I'm just hear to enjoy a couple beers with my friend, so why don't you just calm down?'"

"But did you notice how she went out of her way to talk to you, to have a long conversation with you, so that you, as my friend, would like her? Did you see that?"

"Yea, yea, I noticed. You're becoming annoying. You better not act this giddy around her or she'll think you like her."

"She knows I like her. But I try not to reveal how much I like her because I think it'll make her uncomfortable."

"Of course it will, man. Trust me, I know how it is. You can't be too desperate, but you can't be too distant." As he said this, he spread his arms akimbo and moved his hands up and down as if weighing desperation and distance. He sneered. "They always act like that," Eddie said. "But I don't let them get away with it when they try to do it to me. I just take their bullshit and give it right back to them."

"How do you mean, Eddie?"

"Oh, women today are pathetic, with juggling their particular definition of independence against whatever quote unquote time of their life it is and their father's example. It's all bullshit. You just avoid it all if you don't let them know you like them. Are there any things you don't understand about her, or your relationship with her?" I told him some of the aspects of it that were puzzling to me.

"Oh yea," Eddie said. "She's playing games."

"She said she didn't like playing games."

"Ha. That's a lie. All girls like playing games, man. It's part of it. You have to learn to love the games so you can use them to your advantage. And the only way you can do that is by not appearing to like her."

"Well, Eddie, I'm not sure if I can do that."

I was so happy when I was with her. I delighted in those aspects of a relationship which perhaps color every romantic relationship. I cherished the confidential compliments we exchanged, the idea that we were together against all mathematical and social odds, and the affectionate caresses. I grinned when we had time to go about in public. Other guys ogled her and made advances and I knew that they had no chance with her because of me. The idea that a beautiful woman could take a taxi to be with me or prepare food for me filled me with elation and wonder.

But I also admired Albertine for her own characteristics. She smelled of her shampoo instead of some prissy perfume and the accents and intonations of her voice were pleasant to my ears. We could discuss politics or books and talk all night not as lovers but as two intelligent people who liked each other's company. She had a sensible soul for my mad one and a salve for my insecurities. There is something so beautiful about the smile that a woman reserves only for her lover. I couldn't believe my good fortune. I knew then, as I know now, that I was in love with her.

There was a lot of love in that office. It was easy to tell in those last few days, and, if people were afraid to show it too much, Reggie wasn't. He told everyone that we were his second grandchildren and that he loved every one of us. He put a smile on everyone's face every day.

I remember when we were canvassing near 15th and K, and a waspy guy came up and asked Reggie in a patronizing tone, "So why do you believe in Obama?" The kid looked like he had just come from the Heritage Foundation.

"Because I believe he's gonna change things," Reggie said. "He's gonna get us health care and jobs, and that's gonna be good for me and my kids and everyone. Plus, I don't want any of that damn lipstick on a pit bull."

The guy must have been on the debate team in high school, because he thought he saw an opening.

"That's sexist," he said to Reggie.

"No it ain't," Reggie said. "And I'll say whatever the hell I please. I fought in Vietnam for this country and I don't give a damn what you think of me!" The guy's face turned red, and he had nothing more to say. And I wished then that every Heritage Foundation fuck who thinks this country needs to be set up so that the rich pay no taxes and the only government we have is a military-industrial complex were subjected to some sort of public embarrassment for the damage their ideas have caused. At least one of them had been, thanks to Reggie.

I'll remember Reggie for a lot more than that. On one of the last days, he asked to talk to me.

"I was wondering something," he said. "Is everyone going to remember me after I'm gone?" His eyes were filling and I told him the truth, that nobody would forget him. On reflection, I know now that Reggie saw what was ahead. He understood that Election Day would come and go, and we all would go our separate ways.

On that day, though, I told him that nobody was going to forget him. I set about proving it. His birthday fell on Halloween, the last day of DNC canvassing, and I prepared a book for him as a gift. I had everyone in the office write a note to him to let him know what he meant to them, and I could tell he liked it by the way his eyes lit up. He went around thanking everyone, shaking all the guy's hands warmly and giving all the women hugs.

We all celebrated that night by going to a Halloween party. This one was special because it was the end of our time at PFI. We celebrated each other. But we all knew the real celebration was coming four days later.

Chapter 18

From The Fiddler of Dooney

For the good are always the merry,
Save by an evil chance.
And the merry love the fiddle.
And the merry love to dance.

-W.B. Yeats

Election Night wasn't what I thought it would be. I had visualized ninety-six hours of door knocking, phone calling, poll watching, precinct supervising, and nail biting until the results would find me inebriated and exhausted in some place I never would have imagined myself. I figured Progressive Futures Incorporated could make some or all of this vision come true. Instead, I got a conference call telling me to prepare the office for a change to Save the Children.

It was a relief at the time. I had circled November 4th as the day I would no longer be an employee of PFI, no longer subject to the tedium of my tasks and responsibilities as a director. I was correct on those points. I didn't know that I would also lose the friendships of the people I was working with, the confidence that comes from leadership, and the esteem of the woman with whom I had fallen in love. Had I been able to grasp these additional losses, I wouldn't have protested my plight so much. I wouldn't have repeated "I can't wait until Election Day" over and over again. I would have celebrated every minute of the final days.

A lot of my new friends expressed interest in getting out the vote. It seemed odd to them, as it did to me, that our office should wind down before the election was over. Albertine and I visited the Arlington Obama headquarters, which was overflowing with eager volunteers. An organizer there handed us a map to a place called Warrenton, Virginia, and told us they needed bodies out there.

The next morning, we picked up two of our other friends from the office, Tom and Lindsay, and drove out there in my Rav-4. The Obama headquarters and the houses where we reminded people to vote that day were hard to find, but it was a beautiful fall day. It was inspiring to drive in rural Virginia, in "real" Virginia, and find Obama supporters, but the work was not satisfying. We were handing out doorknob placards with the polling location written on them and reminding people to vote on Tuesday. This kind of canvassing had neither the risk nor payoff we were used to, and a little yipping dog bit me on the ankle. The Obama office was impressive, though. Every canvasser had a sophisticated map and a system to keep track of their responses, and we were four of about thirty people who showed up to canvass. One of the Obama organizers told me that if Obama won half of Falquier County, he would run away with the state. Since John Kerry would not have had any kind of presence in such a location in 2004, the office was a testament to the resources of the campaign and the willingness of people all around the country to work in their neighborhoods on behalf of Barack Obama.

A moment from that day still warms my heart. I was backing the Rav-4 out of the last driveway, and, as I used the rear view mirror to find my way, caught sight of Albertine, her voluminous floppy brown hair let down to her shoulders and her eyes shining against the backdrop of a burning amber rural dusk. I looked away, afraid to be caught staring. But I stole another glance and saw her smiling at me in full endorsement of my earlier gaze. I grinned back, wishing that I could back the Rav-4 all the way back to Arlington to keep the expressions we exchanged intact. I wish I were backing that Rav-4 out of the driveway right now, but the memory of it will remain with me as long as I live.

On Monday, the day before the election, Obama made his final campaign stop in Manassas, Virginia. A larger group from our office went to the rally, and my Rav-4 was one in a caravan. The speech was scheduled for 9 p.m., but we left Arlington in the early afternoon to beat the traffic. There was no beating the traffic. We parked miles away from the Manassas Fairgrounds where Obama would be speaking and trudged in packs that would soon form into lines inching toward the entrance. It took almost an hour to find our place, but we were able to loop around where the incline of the dusty grounds gave us a sight line to the podium. When we found this spot around dusk, the rest of the grounds and the hill beyond the complex fences were empty. By the time night had come, though, the complex and the hill were filled with people. Most accounts put the attendance at or near 85,000 people to see the first major black presidential candidate speak near the site of the first battle of the Civil War.

The people around us began to get restless as small drops of rain started falling. Candidates show up late by rule, and this one was no exception. For some reason, the P.A. system played the same six songs over and over. There was no mention of when Sen. Obama would arrive. People began to push through the crowd trying to find friends they had left to use the restroom, and other people didn't believe they had been up front first.

One woman standing beside us wondered whether anyone else would be joining us after the women in our group returned from the bathroom to squeeze back into our spot. I smiled and apologized for the size of our group, explaining what had brought all of us out there. When Obama had spoken and everyone was leaving, that woman who had been annoyed with us earlier grabbed my arm and said, "Thank you for canvassing."

She was emblematic. During the starts of political rallies where it appears the candidate will never appear, it's easy to hear complaining. People can't believe how late it's getting. They start naming times after which they will no longer wait. They start talking about how crowded the roads will be after the event. The test of a political speaker is whether people speak of these matters after he has spoken, and Obama passed that test. Inching back to the car, I didn't hear one complaint. I heard only love for this man, love for fellow attendees, love for what the country could be if Obama were president.

It was his last stump speech, and he delivered it with the charisma that makes people believe in him and makes Republicans gag. He ended with the story on the origin of the call-and-response chant "Fired Up! Ready to Go!" He had woken up sick and grumpy one morning to find a determined woman in South Carolina chanting it. And in the story of the reason for his grumpiness, he built such rapport with the audience that, by the uplifting part where the audience was to join in the chant, everyone in the crowd believed he was like them and would be the kind of president who deserved their belief.

I was one of them. That speech was one of the best moments of my life. As was the drive home, when Albertine and the others fell asleep because they knew they could rest assured that I would navigate the roads and traffic by myself. Albertine had her hand in mine as she slept beside me in the front seat, and I drove with one hand on the steering wheel and wondered if I was living in a dream. I felt more like a man than I ever have before.

And yet, before Obama had come on stage, I was one of the people worrying about trivial matters. I was preoccupied with the idea that the event would run too late for the Metro, just as, during the drive, I worried that I would get lost trying to find my friends' apartments. If I had known then that moments this sweet cannot last, I wouldn't have let insignificant matters into my mind. On that night, I couldn't foresee it. I put my head to pillow understanding the historical significance of the election without understanding the personal significance of its end.

I did need sleep, though. Election Night was a late, great night. We went out to a small bar in Chinatown where we almost had the place to ourselves. By nine p.m., the foregone conclusion had become reality: Barack Obama had won Pennsylvania. It took only a few moments before Sen. McCain gave a gracious concession speech. Obama took the stage in Grant Park a few minutes later. When the speech ended, we paid up our tabs. There was an understanding that we needed to celebrate in the street.

I was about to do just that when I heard Albertine calling. She was sitting by herself at the bar, a drink in front of her and a blank expression on her face.

"This is amazing!" I said. "Can you believe it? We've gotta get out of here and go out with everyone else."

"I think you're too much for me," she said quietly.

"What?" I said, not sure I understood her.

"You're too much."

"Too much? I don't get it."

"This!" She motioned between her and me. "I don't think I can take this. You're too much." Her meaning became clear to me. I stood in silence, flabbergasted.

"Oh, we'll talk about this another time. Forget I said anything. Let's go catch up with everyone else." I attempted to put the episode out of my mind. I didn't succeed. I celebrated like everyone did that night, but Albertine's words would ring in my mind periodically. I was stunned that the same woman who smiled at me in the rear view mirror and fell asleep with her hand in mine could have said this to me at this of all times. Upon reflection, though, Albertine was foolish for not knowing what she wanted, and I was more foolish for believing I could force mutual love where there was none.

A few minutes later, I found myself on the corner of 7th and H screaming my head off for joy. My friend Tom climbed up a light pole, and he was swinging from side to side. We had joined up with another pack of people, and we were waving at the cars that went by with the drivers leaning on their horns and waving back. There were chants of "O-BAM-A! O-BAM-A!" At some point, there was an idea that we should go to the White House. I don't know who suggested it, but I do know I found myself walking down 7th Street high-fiving passersby and bellowing that we had won at the top of my lungs.

Whoever proposed that we go to the White House had a great idea. The space in front was a mass of young people. I'll never forget screaming "Yes we did!" and "Who's house? Barack's house!" and singing "Na na na, hey, hey, hey, goodbye!" and the National Anthem. There was a collective joy on the streets of D.C. that night. It was an elation at the idea that such a candidate, the kind we had professed to believe in before we knew of his existence, could not only exist but could win the White House.

At some point that night, Reggie called me. I hadn't heard the ring, but he left me a voicemail. When I heard it in the morning, it made me weep for its sheer honesty and joy, two qualities that Reggie brought with him everywhere. He was the spirit of this election for me. I wrote his message down word for word.

He said, "We did it! We did it! We're the unsung heroes. We're the grunts in the field, out in the heat, getting cursed out, getting spit on, begging people for money, telling people to volunteer. Everybody voted, and they did their thing, but we were the grunts in the field. But I appreciate what we did because I can see the results. I appreciate and love every minute of it because I can see what we accomplished. Old as I am, y'all are some young people and y'all did it out of your hearts. And I ain't gonna never forget that."

For all the personal significance of Reggie's message, it also sums up the immediate historical significance of the 2008 election. The canvasser, the field director, and the organizer were the ones who won this election. Obama raised the money, and David Plouffe and David Axelrod helped him spend it wisely, but nothing could have been accomplished without a ground game. Thousands of people bought into the concept of a well-oiled machine and their role as a gear in it, and they worked day and night all across the country to see it succeed.

The results are impressive: 53% of the popular vote, the most for any Democrat since LBJ in 1964; wins in every swing state except my home state of Missourah; wins in Virginia, North

Carolina, Florida, and Indiana; and the election of the first African-American President. The course of the Obama presidency will decide whether this represented a mandate to institute liberal policies in the manifold areas where they are needed. If so, 2008 will be taught by history teachers as a realigning election. If the Democratic party can hold on to the gains it made in all demographic groups in this election, it will be in power for a generation.

Observers should note the participation of young people in the 2008 election. It's a constituency that gets run through the mud by commentators who say that the youth vote never turns out and by curmudgeons who don't think young people have the gumption to participate in politics. The magnitude of young people who took part in this election wipes away these views. Young people have always played a crucial role in our political system as protesters and campaign workers, but this election seemed a special illustration. It was young people who spread word of the campaign by mouth and Web, ran the thousands of campaign offices, and celebrated in the streets on Election Night. I felt a sense of accomplishment for everyone my age.

I felt a sense of accomplishment for myself as well. In November of 2007, I was sitting in Sociology class and talking about the problems in our society. There were issues that I researched with fervor in an effort to learn the extent of America's problems, but I never knew satisfaction that I had worked to solve them. After months of working twelve to fourteen-hour days, I am entitled to that claim, or at least the claim that I can work day and night for something I believe in instead of doing what is the furthest from doing something, which is talking.

Epilogue

The Bare Cherry Tree

> The bare cherry tree
> higher than the roof
> last year produced
> abundant fruit. But how
> speak of fruit confronted
> by that skeleton?
> Though live it may be
> there is no fruit on it.
> therefore chop it down
> and use the wood
> against this biting cold.
>
> -William Carlos Williams

The winter after the election was the most difficult season of my life. Less than two months after Election Day, I found myself canvassing on a frigid day just down Wisconsin Avenue from the hotel where I had trained to be a Progressive Futures director in July. Whenever I saw someone approaching me, I would straighten up and greet them with the energy and enthusiasm required for canvassing. I'd become a Save the Children canvasser, and I delivered my new script with a smile. After each conversation, though, I would put my head back down in dejection until the next person came up.

Everyone and everything seemed distant after the election. The winning candidate I celebrated became another office with no interest in my resume. When I signed on to work for Progressive Futures back at Texas, I imagined that my employment with PFI would lead to other opportunities. I was wrong. I had made no connections with that organization. I thought of myself as a part of the winning team, but I didn't know anybody of influence on the Obama campaign.

I submitted my resume to the transition team anyways. I got an email confirmation in receipt of my resume, but then just a constant stream of automatic e-mails, some of which asked me for money for the transition team, a baffling premise. I've never heard of a transition team soliciting donations, and I would never dream of giving money to one.

I am told by those with more experience than I that a job search can dampen one's enthusiasm for anything at times, but I did not anticipate it on election night. I became bitter toward people with comfortable employment and some people who were attempting to be helpful.

Looking for a new job is like trying to get over being dumped in the way that everyone is an expert. They all wanted to give me advice about how to format my resume, reminisce about their own job searches, and promise to put me in touch with acquaintances. Nobody offered the prospect of an interview at a definitive time and place. In the same manner, everyone who heard that Albertine had ended our relationship offered encouraging platitudes and personal experiences. Nobody had a solution.

I didn't see that coming, either. I know now that I was deluding myself, but I never would have foreseen her breaking things off before Thanksgiving. The smile that had attracted me to her in the first place and increased my love for her every day disappeared from her face, never to return. She became a different person to me in the space of a week.

The end came the day I had hoped for a new beginning. I was set to drive back to Kansas City the Sunday before Thanksgiving to celebrate with my parents, and Albertine asked to see me before I left. She repeated that she felt our relationship was too much, said she needed her space, and told me that she wanted to feel independent. Yet, the memory of that morning is not a fully bitter one because I remember the look of profound concern that came over her face.

Out of habit, Albertine continued to call me. I took her calls gladly, and spoke with her as long as she wanted to. Yet, when I took it upon myself to try to arrange a meeting, she would decline or delay the time that we were to meet until it didn't happen.

I did not begin to recover until Albertine asked me not to contact her, a request that came as a relief to me because it released me from hoping to see her again. I only moved on when I was left to my own devices to perceive that the end of our relationship was for the better, that it is not worthwhile to love a person who doesn't make herself available. I was also pleased by her request because of the thought that she had asked me to do something and that I had the opportunity to comply. The thought that there was a way that I could keep myself from shrinking further in her esteem convinced me to agree to her request to the point that she has not had to ask me again. And now, I say and think about Albertine that it's a pleasure just to have known her.

I will do whatever is asked of me by women I believe I can love. I know my willingness to love will lead to more painful experiences in the future, but I know from my experiences with Albertine what sharing the world with another person can mean to me. The pain of losing her is worth it. I know that I am not the first person to fall into the most fecund ditch of all by wooing a proud woman not kindred of my soul. Love will come again for me because what I have to give is pure and sincere and because of the qualities that make me desirable as a person. It will come when I least expect it, from a person I can't imagine as I write these words, at a time that may or may not be convenient to me.

I am resigned to the acuteness and intensity of my feelings. My soul wounds easily, but it's the one I have, and I love it. To paraphrase Rumsfeld, we live life with the nature that we have, not the one we may want. I also know that the periodic pricks of heartsickness I endure have elation as their counterpart, an ecstasy that comes from consuming works of art, by communicating love through words and deeds, and by cataloging the beauty of the world as I live each day. These highs are more frequent than the lows, and I wish to live my life as a demonstration of gratitude for my ability to experience them. I pray for the patience to accept joy as it comes, to avoid thrusting myself at whatever passing fancy that crosses my mind in times of madness. And I yearn to know whether my delusions of grandeur are nearer to the authentic than to the self-indulgent blubberings of a child.

My best season as an athlete was my junior year of high school baseball. I played second base, and I fielded the ground balls that had before been a constant source of anxiety with fluid ease. The fielding of batted balls became like taking the first bite of an apple. I never demanded that the ball be hit to me and I was never surprised when it was. Each ball that touched my glove nestled into the leather with a grace that I could perceive for the split second before my throwing hand found the perfect grip to fire the ball on to the first baseman. I want to live my life the way I played that season. And I want to feel again the happiness of striking a ball straight to the place on the field where it can be of most use to my team.

I wouldn't have known any of this without Albertine. If I see her again, I'll grin my little boy's smile at her in the way that betrays everything I feel for her. It may have quickened our falling out because of the discomfort that my obvious, unequivocal, and immediate love provoked in her, but I'll grin at her all the same because she was the first woman to give part of herself to me and because she eliminated a quadrant of my madness by doing so. And I'll grin at the next beautiful woman I see, too.

Most people I had met during the election disappeared from my life with even greater speed than Albertine. Where before I had been their ring leader, their court jester, their friend, I never saw most of them again. My elders, even people who had been on Earth for only two or three more years than me, knew that I would lose my position in my newfound friends' lives before I had told them. When I talked about the people with whom it was my privilege to share this election, they would ask, with a knowledge of life that astonished me, "Well, everyone probably went their separate ways after the election, huh?" These questions heartened me by the knowledge that others too had experienced times of great joy that did not last.

My friends from Progressive Futures were probably stuck in their own job searches. Mine was hopeless in the immediate aftermath of the election. I had no choice but to return to Progressive Futures as a canvasser. As a regular canvasser for eight hours a day, four days a week, I made $200 to $400 more per week than I did as a director working ten to fourteen hours a day, six and seven days a week.

I got commission because I was still an effective canvasser, even a better one. Every day I went back out to the streets, I brought a politeness people couldn't help but respond to and a persistence that would convince at least one person a day to make monthly contributions to Save the Children, our office's new client. I wore long underwear, two pairs of gloves, a heavy jacket, a tight-fitting stalking cap with ear flaps, and a pair of heavy Timberland boots, and I got used to my mouth being too frozen to talk at the end of the day. Since every day depended on running into the right person at the right time, I didn't stop canvassing for lunch, lest I miss that person. My efforts were rewarded every day by people who allowed me to convince them to sacrifice a minute of frostbite to give to a great cause.

There were rare days when I couldn't convince anyone to become a monthly sponsor, but most days I knew I could find one person who wanted to make monthly donations if I kept a smile on my face and stayed out there all day. Without the benefit of an election to stir my interest, most of my arguments with possible donors were not based on reasonable appeals, but rather on my ability to convince them to use their credit card information on the street with me today instead of at a later date at home on their computers. I always found one person, even on that day on Wisconsin Avenue when I became maudlin.

I repeated lines of Yeats to myself again and again to cope with my circumstances, but I also thought often of the Flannery O'Connor short story about the Bible salesman who seduces a one-legged woman who lives with her parents in a small Southern town. After the salesman has sold the premium edition to her parents, and after she makes love to him in the loft of an abandoned barn, the one-legged woman reveals that, like the nihilists she has read while cooped up in her parents' house, she believes in nothing. The salesman seems awed by the idea, and he asks her if she will allow him to see her without her wooden leg. She doesn't want to at first, but relents after he continues to ask in his prettiest words. After she detaches the leg, though, the salesman immediately grabs the leg and climbs down from the loft, pulling the ladder down after him. He then picks up her belongings and heads for the door. And as he is leaving, he turns around and says, "Oh, by the way, I've believed in nothing since the day I was born."

As I gave people my "aw-shucks" smile and my guilt-trip inducing requests for financial support, I felt sometimes that I was this Bible salesman, using a good cause to make a buck. As morbid as that thought was, it allowed me to ignore the many people who had the audacity to bear ill will to me while I was fighting child poverty in the freezing cold.

There were still those times of affirmation that make canvassing a magical experience. One Saturday, the mall shoppers of the Columbia Heights area did not seem very interested in talking about Save the Children's efforts to combat the lack of education and health care that breeds poverty. Most were more inclined to see if Target or Best Buy had the product they were looking for. I kept my charm offensive alive all day nonetheless, and I had accepted a few cash donations, an amount far short of what I would need to raise on a Saturday to ensure that my canvassing average would be high enough to make a living wage for the week. Finally, a small Filipino woman said, "Sure, I will do it," when I asked if she had a minute for Save the Children. As I was delivering my rap, she interrupted me to ask if I had eaten dinner. When I shook my head, she led me around the corner to a Chinese restaurant and told me to order anything on the menu, her treat. "Today," she said, smiling, "I feel rich." She had just moved to D.C. from her native country and felt blessed to have a job helping neighborhood children learn to read. After signing up to be a Save the Children sponsor, she told me how she did so because she wanted to help young girls get the education she was denied when she was young. She said I was doing God's work, and I won't forget her.

That interaction was my favorite, but others stand out, like the time a grocery sacker crossed himself before handing me the crumpled $100 bill he had labored for days in our stingy, debilitating economy to earn. I won't forget him either.

On the other hand, one woman I met didn't forget me. I was canvassing in Dupont on a dreary Sunday in January when I ran into the middle-aged black woman with cropped hair who had given me $20 for the DNC and wonderful complements on my first good day canvassing in Silver Spring so many months before. She recognized me before I remembered her, but she told me about how she had canvassed door to door in her neighborhood and cried on election night. These stories would have been enough by themselves to fill me once more with the love of the goodness of the people we speak to every day as it is manifested in canvassing, but she also decided to give $30 a month to Save the Children.

These were the best times I had canvassing for Save the Children. The worst times were the ones when I realized the hypocrisy of advocating for starving children in Africa when there were homeless and penniless people sitting and walking by me. The surroundings of Union Station, one of my frequent canvassing spots, are filled with people driven to poverty and mental imbalance by our country's economy. Every time I canvassed by Union Station I saw a hunched over woman dragging a rolling suitcase behind her quivering gait and a man wearing only an old wrinkled suit in the frigid weather, muttering to nobody and everyone, "They took my home. They took my home." And I stood in the shadow of our Capitol and guilt-tripped Hill staffers and government employees into becoming members of Save the Children.

One day in Chinatown, a homeless man kept walking by me to berate me. I didn't ask him if he had one minute for Save the Children for obvious reasons, but he kept approaching me.

"Gimme some money," he said. I told him that I was sorry, that I didn't have any to give.

"Yes, you do," he said. "Look at those gloves. You paid for them didn't you? Look at my hands. I ain't got any gloves." Not knowing how to respond, I told him sorry again, and repeated that I didn't have anything to give.

"Would you say the same thing if I pulled a gun on you?"

I said I would. That didn't satisfy him, and he began to demand that I deliver my rap to him. I refused, and he said that he would, in that case, just stand there, that it was a public area and he could stand wherever he wanted to. Then he began to pee on himself, and the urine flowed out of his pant leg and became a puddle on the sidewalk. The noxious smell of it pervaded me. I couldn't and didn't want to do anything to him, and I was determined to find my sponsor, so I just walked away. Later in the day, I signed up a sponsor standing on the exact spot where he had urinated. I knew because there was a stain on the sidewalk where the puddle had been.

The winter seemed to be a refutation of everything that I believed I had achieved in life. I felt I had done as I was told my entire life, made every grade my parents, teachers, and I pressured me to achieve, learned every lesson my relations and mentors had taught me, done everything I was supposed to do. But there was no payoff. I heard back from no organization that I emailed my resume, and I read newspaper stories about the worst recession since the Great Depression. I felt a sense of inferiority to the people who snubbed me on their way by, the people who were less intelligent than me and worked less hard than me yet commanded more respect from society. I fumed at the conversations about insignificant matters that I interrupted to ask if anyone had a minute for Save the Children and hated the people who responded to my question as if it were a violation of the rules of propriety. But I never thought of leaving D.C. I took deep breaths of the clean cold air and clasped my hands together palm in palm once more like an obedient student of the Master, and I smiled at the next passerby.

I still found beauty on the Metro. There is something awe-inspiring in the hot stench of those train tracks and the rumbling of those trains. There is something humbling in the way the updraft of an approaching train obliges a career woman to hold her long skirt so it doesn't fly. There is something remarkable in a car filled with people who are so diligent that they check their e-mails and evaluate grant requests on their way home from work. And there is beauty in the diversity of the human race.

My other employment increased my desire to make it in DC. Through a high school acquaintance, I secured an internship in a senator's office on the Hill two days a week. I dressed in what formal clothes I had, and I answered the office phone on Tuesdays and Thursdays. Most of the calls were from irate constituents who had just heard Rush Limbaugh say something stupid or watched an erroneous Fox News report. They called in to express frustration with the right's political fate and with their own lives, bemoaning the "people like you who have it so easy up there in Washington." I listened with patience and politeness until they stopped talking. Then I made false promises to let the senator know what they said.

Inauguration was amazing yet also painful. I decided to make some extra money by hawking Obama merchandise to the tourists who mobbed the town. I saw all the ideals I fought for so hard all election season reduced to shitty pairs of earrings with

Barack Obama's face on them. "Would you like a pair of OOOObama flair?" I asked passersby outside the National Mall in an obtrusive voice. "Barack Obama earrings, get 'em right here!" I made enough money, but it was awful to stand alone again as a salesman when I should have been celebrating with the people who had elected our 44th President.

Nothing could have ruined Inauguration Day. I was standing near the Washington Monument in the midst of a crowd of 2 million people. I took nips of whiskey and yelled my head off and laughed and wept with those around me. I vowed that Inauguration would be my last association with the 2008 election, and that I would stop wishing that it were October.

Yet, Obama's election remains a constant source of joy to me. I have plastered my bedroom wall with magazine pictures of him and the first family that America has fallen in love with, and I support the gradual way he is attempting to cope with our nation's troubles. I've also put up crew sheets from Progressive Futures with canvasser's names and fundraising totals for particular days because I think of them every time I think of Obama, and it is pleasing to see their names written in their own handwriting.

There is no question that I worked with great people and learned a great deal about myself. The experience had unquestionable value. The question in my mind is whether PFI and organizations of its kind are beneficial to progressive politics. My office was effective, raising over a million dollars during my time there. We also did the important work of acting as the public face of the party. We started conversations with people they would bring up during dinner at home that night, and I believe our presence on the streets was a reminder that there were a number of ways for ordinary people to get involved in the election. I've said all along that the people who gave us money would vote Democratic, but they would also take an ownership stake in the election. Their contribution made them more likely to keep themselves abreast of current events, more likely to encourage friends and neighbors to vote Democratic, and more likely to get involved again next election season. This has value, as does the manner that groups like Progressive Futures provide a meeting ground for young progressives who learn the nuts and bolts of running a campaign office and learn that they are not the only ones their age concerned about the course of world events. My time at PFI did not net me a job immediately after the election, but it might in the future.

There are also, it is obvious, worrisome aspects of PFI and groups like it. I am not aware of the people who profit at this for-profit corporation. They certainly were not my immediate supervisors, who were compensated just as poorly as I was. Somewhere, there might be a progressive who has discovered a way to make money by fundraising for good causes like the Democratic Party and Save the Children. It ought to take place in the light of day. There is an individual or group of individuals who has set up this mechanism by which you can fight for others to earn a living wage while not earning one yourself, yet laws are supposed to exist to keep people from working for less than minimum wage or to keep people from being misled by their employer. My biggest concern with my time at PFI was the damage done to the lives of people who believed they could better their penurious financial situations by working for Progressive Futures. My actions exacerbated their problems. It's unclear whether PFI's clients are aware or have anything to say about the way the company treats its employees. There is a place in progressive politics for groups like Progressive Futures, but there must be a way for the groups' functions to be disclosed and a way to ensure adequate treatment for employees.

Every time I worked in that senatorial office, I went to a Cosi near the Hill for a bagel and coffee in the morning. And every time I went there, I saw a strange old woman who would approach me and relate in an accent the story of a man who was trying to ruin her life. I think she took a special liking toward me.

"Vat book are you reading?" she asked one morning. I showed her.

"Vauw! You ah a thinkaa, maan!" she exclaimed.

Another day, she appeared frustrated with me.

"You come here every Tuesday and Thursday, don't you?" she asked. I nodded.

"You ah a very disciplined person," she said. "But you ah extremely difficult to read. I have known you for several weeks now, and I know very little about you."

"I get that a lot," I told her.

This is where I'll end my account of the 2008 election. I still believe it has the potential to be a realigning moment. I'm still in D.C. because I want to see the Obama Administration succeed, and I want to help shift our government to the left. I would like to see the United States become a socialist democracy like much of Europe. I want our nation's soldiers out of Iraq and Afghanistan, and I want to see Guantanamo, Abu Gharib, and Bagram closed. I want the Patriot Act repealed. I want high-quality health care, education, and the Internet to be available to all Americans, regardless of race or wealth. I want to see high speed rail built in all of our cities and all across the country, and fuel-efficient cars dotting our roads. I want everyone in this country to have access to the benefits of marriage regardless of sexual orientation. I want the death penalty abolished. I want everyone to pay taxes according to his or her income, not according to their ability to hire accountants who know loopholes. And I want to see pot decriminalized.

You might think I'm radical, but you must admit that I know I can work my ass off in the pursuit of these goals. The people who ran America into the ground in the opening years of this century have made the mistake of getting old before they got wise. And if you continue to complain about the taxes on your capital gains, or squirm about the end of white male American dominance of the world, know that I consider you my opponent, and know that I will be doing whatever I can to see you beaten.